LANGUAGE IS SERVED

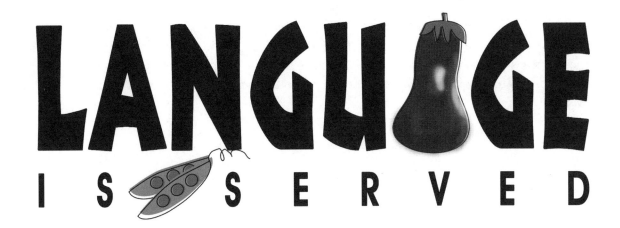

GAMES, WRITING PROMPTS, AND OTHER LANGUAGE ARTS ACTIVITIES ON THE YUMMY TOPIC OF FOOD

CHERYL MILLER THURSTON

Cottonwood Press, Inc.
Fort Collins, Colorado

Requests for special permission should be addressed to:

Cottonwood Press, Inc.
109-B Cameron Drive
Fort Collins, Colorado 80525

E-mail: cottonwood@cottonwoodpress.com
Web: www.cottonwoodpress.com
Phone: 1-800-864-4297
Fax: 970-204-0761

ISBN: 978-1-877673-79-5

Printed in the United States of America

TABLE OF CONTENTS

(For a listing of activities categorized by topic, see the topic index, page 151.)

TABLE OF CONTENTS (CONTINUED)

INTRODUCTION: INTRODUCTION: INTRODUCTION:

Because it is essential to our lives, food makes a good subject for classroom activities. It is familiar to everyone. Everyone has something to say about it. It can arouse strong feelings. It is part of our daily lives, yet it also plays an important role in special events, like birthday parties, camping trips, wedding receptions, and Fourth of July barbecues.

We all have opinions about food and just about everything related to it. There is cooking—our own and the cooking of others. There is fast food, gourmet food, health food, junk food, and ethnic food. There is school cafeteria food, restaurant food, airplane food, and the "food" you buy to snack on at the movie theater. There are important questions to settle, like what *exactly* should go on a good hot dog, and should you ever, ever put salt on a cantaloupe or refrigerate a tomato?

In *Language Is Served,* food plays a prominent role in some activities. In others, it plays only a minor role. The activities are quite varied, with topics appearing in no particular order. (English teachers tend to need things in no particular order. One day they may be looking for a quick lesson on verbs, the next for something on vocabulary, and the next for a writing topic. Some days, only a word game will fill the bill—something that will wake students up to paying attention to the English language.) To help you find an activity that addresses a certain skill or topic, please see the topic and subtopic index on page 151.

Many of the activities in the book involve games and creativity. That's because I think *playing* with language is so crucial to building language skills. Students need to develop an interest in words and their quirkiness, versatility, and power. English teachers need to do all they can to turn kids *on* to language. Play has power.

Although my name is on the book as its official author, it is not my efforts alone that have made it possible. Samantha Prust and Sarah Stimely worked alongside me and assisted in so many ways—writing, proofreading, fact-checking, you name it. Thank you also goes to Heather Madigan, Mary Gutting, and Anne Marie Martinez, who all helped in a variety of ways.

I hope you enjoy *Language is Served* and find it useful in your classroom.

Cheryl Miller Thurston

Name _____

HEALTHY SCRAMBLING

Unscramble all of the foods below. They are all foods that might be part of a healthy diet.

1. briwaserters _____
2. turgoy _____
3. culttee _____
4. ciknech _____
5. shif _____
6. rotcars _____
7. kilm _____
8. rebda _____
9. frugiprate _____
10. madslon _____
11. alcree _____
12. stapa _____
13. sgeg _____
14. nionos _____
15. shormomus _____
16. sepalojan _____
17. zorgaban nabes _____
18. acheeps _____
19. volesi _____
20. ochaterski _____
21. elan korp _____
22. der repepp _____
23. crumbcue _____
24. ignerg _____
25. grusasapa _____
26. abasnan _____
27. futo _____

28. crobicol _____
29. chinaps _____
30. saym _____
31. sargone _____
32. pepsal _____
33. calgri _____
34. elovi loi _____
35. motetosa _____
36. yertuk _____
37. eslirubereb _____
38. tebes _____
39. seburssl upsorst _____
40. nupres _____
41. narsisi _____
42. malaeto _____
43. sepatoot _____
44. werficaulol _____
45. snikmupp _____
46. wornb cire _____
47. galptneg _____
48. ronc _____
49. niprut segren _____
50. yabler _____

"Health food
makes me sick."

—Calvin Trillin

Name _____

CHOCOLATE MASHED POTATOES

What food stories are told in your family? Do you talk about a time when everything went wrong with a special dinner or a special dish? Do you all reminisce about your late great-grandmother's wonderful homemade ravioli? Did something funny happen to your brother at a restaurant? Do you laugh at how you all hated to eat at your mom's best friend's house when you were younger—all because she drowned everything in really awful gray gravy?

One Seattle man always tells his grandchildren about the time his mom was away from home and his dad cooked dinner. He was getting ready to mash the potatoes when he discovered they were out of milk. They had chocolate milk, though, so he made the potatoes with that. They turned out brown, and his son still talks about those chocolate mashed potatoes.

Write about a food story shared in your family. Talk to relatives if you need some help thinking of one. If you can't think of anything at all, share any kind of memory you have of an occasion that involved food—maybe a special birthday meal, the time you got food poisoning, the pumpkins you grew in your backyard, etc.

"All I really need is love, but a little chocolate now and then doesn't hurt!"

—Lucy Van Pelt in *Peanuts* by Charles M. Schulz

Name _____

SYLLABLE CHALLENGE

 How many one-syllable foods can you list? How many two-syllable foods? Three-syllable foods? Four-syllable foods?

Give yourself one point for every one-syllable food, two points for every two-syllable food, three points for every three-syllable food, and four points for every four-syllable food. Each food must be only one word (no two-word foods like *hot dog*). See if you can score at least 100 points.

The lists below will help you get started.

ONE-SYLLABLE FOODS	TWO-SYLLABLE FOODS	THREE-SYLLABLE FOODS	FOUR-SYLLABLE FOODS
1. soup	1. waffle	1. banana	1. huckleberry
2. milk	2. spinach	2. potato	2. cauliflower

"Our language is funny—a fat chance and a slim chance are the same thing."

—J. Gustav White

Name _____

HELP HUNGRY HENRY'S

Read through the menu below.

HUNGRY HENRY'S FOOD SHACK

ENTREES		SIDES	
Meat Loaf	$6.00	Mashed Potatoes	$4.00
Fried Chicken	$5.00	Fries	$3.00
Hamburger	$4.00	Green Beans	$2.00
Hot Dog	$3.00	Coleslaw	$1.00

There isn't anything fancy about this menu. It's completely straightforward and clear.

It's also rather boring. Maybe that's why Hungry Henry's Food Shack hasn't been doing well since it opened up, even though people who have eaten there say it's the best food they have ever tasted. The employees at Hungry Henry's think the problem is the lackluster menu.

Help Hungry Henry's Food Shack drum up some business by adding some pizzazz to their menu. Rename each item. Then use vivid descriptions to make each one sound like the most delicious dish ever created. Remember to use complete sentences. The more specific details you add, the better. The first one is done for you in the example below.

EXAMPLE

Mom's Meat Loaf
This extraordinary meat loaf made of premium quality meats is seasoned and sauced to perfection, sliced thick, and covered in mouth-watering gravy—just like Mom used to make.

"Red meat is not bad for you. Now blue-green meat, *that's* bad for you!"

—Tommy Smothers

DON'T KNOCK IT UNTIL YOU TRY IT

Every culture has its own food traditions. The foods people find appetizing in the U.S. are not always considered tasty in other parts of the world. Likewise, foods that people enjoy in other countries sometimes seem downright disgusting to those growing up in America.

The items below are foods enjoyed by people in different countries all over the world. Using the Internet, find out about each of the foods. Then, for each one, write a description from the point of view of someone who thinks the food is incredibly delicious.

EXAMPLE

takosu (slices of boiled octopus soaked in rice vinegar)
Just looking at a dish of takosu makes my mouth water. The premium slices of tender octopus are perfectly marinated in tangy, fresh rice vinegar. The vinegar gives just the right sparkle to the tastebuds and enhances the naturally delicious flavor of the octopus.

1. hakarl

2. scrapple

3. escargot

4. chitterlings

5. poi

6. haggis

7. lutefisk

8. kimchi

"We are living in a world today where lemonade is made from artificial flavors and furniture polish is made from real lemons."

—Alfred E. Newman

Name _____

HUNGER

Hunger is a problem all over the world. In some places there are only small pockets of hunger. In other parts of the world, hunger is widespread.

Below are 10 organizations that, at the time this was written, are all working to help with the problem of hunger in the world. Imagine that you are in charge of an organization that has decided to donate $10,000 each to two different groups. You are in charge of recommending which groups should get the money.

Using the Internet and/or other sources, find out about the groups below. Which two will you choose? Why? Make your selections and then write a 1-2 page report to your organization, explaining why you have chosen these two groups. It is important that the board members agree that the money is to be used wisely, so be as clear as possible about your reasons for choosing these two groups and not others.

Some questions you might use to help evaluate the organizations: Who do they help? What kinds of help do they provide? How do they provide the help?

Note: You may also choose an organization that is not on the list below. Just be sure to give the web site for the organization.

Friends of the World Food Program: www.friendsofwfp.org

Project Peanut Butter: www.projectpeanutbutter.org

Save the Children: www.savethechildren.org

America's Second Harvest: www.secondharvest.org

The Hunger Site: www.thehungersite.com

Bread for the World: www.bread.org

Heifer International: www.heifer.org

Meds & Food for Kids: www.medsandfoodforkids.org

Feed the Children: www.feedthechildren.org

CARE: www.care.org

"If you can't feed a hundred people, then feed just one."

—Mother Teresa

BEWARE OF "BECAUSE"

Because is a perfectly good word, of course. So why should we "beware" of it? It's because it's easy to write a sentence fragment when you use the word *because*. Does that mean you shouldn't use *because?* Absolutely not. It just means that you need to use it correctly.

Here's a sentence fragment: **Because Duke loved Spam.**

He did *what* because he loved Spam? We don't know. The item is not a complete sentence. It needs to have material added to the beginning or the end, like this: **Duke ordered eight cases because he loved Spam.** Or: **Because he loved Spam, Duke ordered eight cases.**

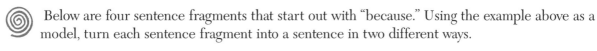 Below are four sentence fragments that start out with "because." Using the example above as a model, turn each sentence fragment into a sentence in two different ways.

1. **Because she hated seeing Gil chew with his mouth open.**

   Add something to the beginning:_____

   _____

   Add something to the end: _____

   _____

2. **Because he wanted to grow perfect watermelons.**

   Add something to the beginning:_____

   _____

   Add something to the end:_____

   _____

3. **Because she wanted to go to medical school someday.**

   Add something to the beginning:_____

   _____

   Add something to the end: _____

   _____

4. **Because of the bug floating in his chocolate shake.**

   Add something to the beginning:_____

   _____

   Add something to the end: _____

   _____

"When those waiters ask me if I want some fresh ground pepper, I ask if they have any aged pepper."

—Andy Rooney

Name _____

SIZZLING SYNONYMS

Synonyms are words that have the same or nearly the same meaning. They add variety and spice to our language. Imagine how boring it would be if we described absolutely everything we liked as "nice," for example. Because of synonyms, we can also describe them as "friendly" or "appetizing" or "pleasant" or "kind," or we can choose from dozens of other synonyms.

Write a synonym for each of the words below, using a thesaurus for help. Then use each synonym in a sentence about food. Try to make the sentences as *interesting* (or *fascinating, entertaining,* or *engaging*) as possible.

1. good
2. spicy
3. crunchy
4. raw
5. sweet
6. frozen
7. thick
8. crisp
9. dark
10. strong
11. warm
12. chewy
13. lumpy
14. cold
15. bland
16. weak
17. dry
18. spoiled
19. sour
20. runny
21. creamy
22. soggy
23. soft
24. light
25. tasteless

"A synonym is a word you use when you can't spell the other one."

—Baltasar Gracián

Name _____

D-D-DOUG'S D-D-DELIGHT

Doug Dougenhoffer has just opened a gourmet restaurant in Denver. He is calling it, unfortunately, Doug Dougenhoffer's Denver Dining Delight. Doug is fascinated with alliteration—the repetition of a consonant sound. He has decided to name the dishes in his restaurant alliteratively. He wants a short radio ad introducing his restaurant to be alliterative, too. (Doug sometimes doesn't display the greatest judgment in the world.)

Help Doug out. Name 10 menu items for his restaurant. (Remember that it's a gourmet place— no chili dogs or potato chips!) You don't have to choose "d" for your alliteration, though Doug would probably appreciate it.

Whatever letter you choose, use the same one to write an alliterative radio ad that will introduce Doug Dougenhoffer's Denver Dining Delight.

"A gourmet is just a glutton with brains."

—P.W. Haberman, Jr.

FIXER UPPER

Here is a real workout for your proofreading and spelling skills. Below is a restaurant review written by a newspaper reporter who clearly needs to brush up on some skills. Well, actually, he needs to do more than brush up. He needs intense writing therapy. Please help out this poor guy by fixing all the errors in his story.

A Grate Place too Eat

The Flamboyant Plum is truely a delightful restraunt, I loved it form the frist byte to the last. The name of the palace comes form the gaint paynting of a plum in the loby. "Flamboyant" discribes the owner Miss. Allexandra Albright a woman who dreses in brite pruple close at all times, she also wheres alot of sequins and stuff. And realy high heals.

All of the food and drinks that are served at the Flamboyant Plum are vegatarian and everything is fresh, well-prepared, and served very attractively on big, huge sqware plaits with pruple flours paynted on them. For appetizers, I expescially loved the artichoke dip with olives imported from france, I also loved the plate of Crackers and Cheese.

When it comes to the main dishes served at the Flamboyant plum you cant go wrong. Miss Albrights brocolli quiche is light and tastey and her goat cheeze dumplings are a spechul treet for anyone who likes goat cheeze dumplings and I do. I frist had them on december 26 2005 at a littel place in albany new york and I couldn't beleive how good they were, I liked them so much I ate six servings. All the main dishes are served with a garden salad and your choice of home made bisquits or or home made bluebery muffens. However you can also order wheat roles instead.

For desert, the choices are amazing. Six different deserts that feature choclate. Five kinds of fruit pie. There are several kinds of pudding and also ice cream. Seven flavors. Ive sampled seven of the deserts and the chocolate green bean pie is the only one that is not quiet wonderful.

Do'nt delay. Take your famly to the Flamboyant Plum this week. Youll be glad you did.

"Proofread carefully to see if you any words out."

—Author Unknown

PASSIVE SENTENCES MUST NOT BE WRITTEN BY YOU

Writing is often stronger when the verbs are in **active voice.** Verbs are in active voice when the subject of the sentence performs the action of the sentence. They are in **passive voice** when the subject receives the action of the sentence instead of performing it.

It sounds complicated, but you can probably hear the difference very easily. Here is a sentence in active voice:

She ordered a pizza with disgusting anchovies.

"She" is the subject of the sentence, and "she" is doing the ordering. Here is how the sentence sounds when it is in passive voice:

A pizza with disgusting anchovies was ordered by her.

Now "pizza" is the subject, but the verb is "was ordered." The subject is not performing the action. Here's another example:

Active: *Mom likes green olives more than black olives.*
Passive: *Green olives are liked by Mom more than black olives.*

Notice that the passive sentences sound rather awkward in the examples above. In most cases, active voice is a much better choice than passive voice.

 Turn the passive sentences below into active ones.

1. The tray of gooey cheese nachos was spilled by Joe all over Mom's new white silk dress.
2. Candy bars were hidden all over the house by Margaret.
3. Sticks of butter were devoured by Tony's strange new neighbor.
4. Bugs are eaten by almost all little children at some time or other.
5. Chocolate covered ants are considered to be delicious by some people.
6. Bananas are eaten whole by monkeys.
7. A great source of protein is bugs.
8. A giant taco salad that was eaten for lunch by him made him sick.
9. The plastic wading pool was filled with grape Kool-Aid by Charles.
10. Aunt Alice's broccoli and chocolate tofu shakes were not liked by any of the five-year-olds at the birthday party.

In the U.S., anchovies always rank last on the list of favorite pizza toppings.

Name _____

CRAZY CORNUCOPIA

Thanksgiving scenes commonly feature a cornucopia, that strange spiral cone "thingy" with all kinds of foods spilling out of it. It has been used as a symbol of abundance for centuries, and that "thingy" was originally a goat's curved horn.

Now why on earth would someone put fruit and grain inside a goat's horn as a symbol of abundance? According to Greek mythology, the god Cronos swallowed his children at birth. (Why? The gods and goddesses of ancient mythology did a lot of strange things!) At any rate, the mother of Zeus tricked Cronos by wrapping up a rock for him to swallow and giving the baby to a nymph named Amalthea to raise. She raised him on the milk of a goat, and Zeus was grateful. When he grew up, he gave Amalthea the goat's horn, with special powers added. Whoever possessed it would receive anything he or she wished for.

That was the start of the cornucopia as a symbol of abundance.

⊚ A goat's horn seems a bit dated for this century. Design your own cornucopia out of something *other* than a goat's horn. What will you use instead for your symbol of abundance? And what will you fill it with? Draw a picture or use photos cut from magazines to create your cornucopia and the items it will contain.

⊚ Then write a paragraph describing your updated cornucopia. What did you choose for the symbol, and why? What does it contain? Why?

A woman picking through frozen turkeys at a grocery store, trying to find one large enough: Do these turkeys get any bigger?
Grocer: No, ma'am. They're dead.

Name _____

WRITE A FOOD AUTOBIOGRAPHY

Most autobiographies include information about where the writer was born, where he or she went to school, and other details about the writer's childhood. A twist on that approach is to write a "food" autobiography. With a food autobiography, the writer tells the story of his or her life *as it relates to food.*

Write your own food autobiography. Look over the questions in each item below. What memories do they trigger? Choose at least six of the items and answer the questions as thoroughly as possible.

- What are some of your earliest memories involving food? Do family members tell stories about you and food when you were a baby? Did you love squash? Spit out spinach? Throw your peas on the floor?

- What have been your favorite foods at different times in your life? What foods have you hated? Why? Have your opinions changed over time? If so, how?

- What are some food traditions in your family? Do you always celebrate birthdays with seafood lasagna? Do you have pie instead of cake on birthdays? Do you always ask your uncle to bring his special pickled beets to Christmas dinner?

- What food have you felt very brave trying? Did you like it or hate it? Why?

- Are there any foods you will absolutely not eat, no matter what? If so, what are they?

- What funny stories in your life have involved food?

- Has food been involved in any embarrassing situations you have experienced or observed?

- Do you pay attention to what foods are good for you? Do you try to "eat healthy"? Why or why not?

- What is your biggest weakness when it comes to food?

- If you could change something about food in your life, what would it be?

- If you had to describe your life thus far in terms of food, what food would best describe your life? Is your life more like a sandwich or a bowl of fruit? A candy bar or a bowl of corn? Or...? Use your imagination!

"I come from a family where gravy is considered a beverage."

—Erma Bombeck

Name _____

BITS AND PIECES

After Dalton gorged on pigs-in-a-blanket.
The mouth-watering beef jerky display.
Aunt Samantha's awful pumpkin and sausage soup.
The green and purple cottage cheese in the forgotten bowl at the back of the refrigerator.

The items above look like sentences. They start with capital letters. They end in periods. They contain information. However, they are not sentences at all. They are sentence fragments. Each sounds incomplete because something important is missing. After Dalton gorged on pigs-in-a-blanket, what happened? What *about* the green and purple cottage cheese in the forgotten bowl at the back of the refrigerator?

Here are some ways the sentence fragments might be turned into sentences:

After Dalton gorged on pigs-in-a-blanket, he drank a quart of orange juice.

The store owner put the mouth-watering beef jerky display right beside the cash register, hoping customers wouldn't be able to resist.

I hate Aunt Samantha's awful pumpkin and sausage soup.

The green and purple cottage cheese in the forgotten bowl at the back of the refrigerator was so disgusting that T.J. felt sick just looking at it.

  Add information to the sentence fragments below and turn them into sentences. You may add information to the beginning, middle or end of the sentences.

1. Ripe blueberry stains on my fingers.
2. The triple sausage and cheese pizza.
3. Driving his mother crazy by refusing to eat anything at all that was green.
4. Boiled beets in a big blue bowl.
5. A big basket of deep-fried fritters.
6. Pushing the bowl of steamy gruel toward me.
7. A package of red licorice whips.
8. The green bean casserole.
9. One of the hottest peppers on earth.
10. Every vegetable in the universe.
11. Nibbling celery.
12. Shoveling ice cream into his mouth at the birthday party for his friend.
13. The smell of fried onions and garlic.
14. Taking a bite of the beef taco.
15. Boiling.

Do vegetarians eat animal crackers?

COPYCATS

When sentences are all constructed in about the same way, they tend to put readers to sleep. Look at the following paragraph:

We celebrated Mom's birthday last night. We ate at a fancy restaurant. It was called Dominique's Cottage. We did not like it at all. We did not like the snooty waiter. We did not like the stuffy atmosphere. We did not like the music they played. We did not recognize anything on the menu. My brother and I wanted hamburgers. They did not have them. We had to eat chicken cordon bleu. We did not like it. Mom did like her shrimp scampi. Dad liked the steak he ordered. He did not like the price. My brother tipped back in his chair. He fell over. Everyone looked at us. We did not like that, either. The waiter helped him up. He was very mad. You could tell. He didn't say anything, though. We will not be going back.

Rewrite the paragraph above and add some variety. You may combine sentences, leave out words, and rearrange, but don't leave out any of the information. You might try using some of these ideas in your rewrite:

- Start a sentence with an *-ing* phrase (a participle).
  Example: **Putting** a fake smile on her face, Selena tried to be courteous to the very rude customer.

- Connect information with a transition word like *because, after* or *when.*
  Example: We jumped out of the water and into the boat as fast as we could **after** we saw those fins.

- Start a sentence with the word "to" and make an infinitive phrase.
  Example: **To** keep from strangling his son when he came home at 3:00 a.m., Mr. Fisher kept both hands on the cup of coffee he had been filling and refilling for the last three hours.

- Put in an appositive—an interrupting phrase that tells you more about one of the nouns.
  Example: When they looked at the other team's captain, **a young man who was almost seven feet tall,** the Crimson High School Raiders suspected they didn't have a chance at the basketball championship.

Important: There is no one "right" or "wrong" way to rewrite the paragraph. Just strive for a sound that is less choppy when you read it aloud.

What is a cannibal's favorite food?

Pizza with everyone on it.

COOL AS A CUCUMBER

Food is everywhere. We see it sold on the street and advertised on billboards. It is the subject of hundreds of commercials. It is an important part of family traditions and religious rituals. We think about it whenever we're hungry, and often even when we are not. It's no wonder that food is a theme in all kinds of common phrases, proverbs, idioms, clichés, and similes.

Below is a list of 145 common food phrases and sentences. Normally, it is *not* a good idea to use a lot of such phrases and sentences in your writing. But this one time, as a challenge to your brain, write a story using as many of the items as possible. (You may also include other common food phrases that you might know.) Your story should make sense and use a *minimum* of 25 sentences or phrases from the list.

Here's an example of one way to start:

*I was **raking in the dough** at my new job and was **cool as a cucumber**. I ate like a king, lived high on the hog, and thought I was the **greatest thing since sliced bread**. However, soon I found out that I had **bitten off more than I could chew**...*

1. on the gravy train
2. the rest is gravy
3. to milk it for all its worth
4. milk of human kindness
5. There's no use crying over spilled milk.
6. food for thought
7. the greatest thing since sliced bread
8. the major breadwinner
9. living on bread and water
10. Half a loaf is better than none.
11. our daily bread
12. to take the bread out of someone's mouth
13. Is the glass half empty or half full?
14. raking in the dough
15. Too many cooks spoil the broth.
16. When life hands you lemons, make lemonade.
17. polish the apple
18. You're the apple of my eye.
19. to wolf something down
20. a tough cookie
21. caught with your hand in the cookie jar
22. That's the way the cookie crumbles.
23. one smart cookie
24. cream of the crop
25. I heard it through the grapevine.
26. slow as molasses in January
27. the big cheese
28. so cheesy
29. eat like a horse
30. An apple a day keeps the doctor away.
31. Don't bite the hand that feeds you.
32. Don't upset the apple cart.
33. How do you like them apples?
34. comparing apples to oranges
35. Don't bite off more than you can chew.
36. rotten to the core
37. a bad apple
38. the whole enchilada
39. two peas in a pod
40. Wake up and smell the coffee.
41. Don't put all of your eggs in one basket.
42. like walking on eggshells
43. You can't make an omelette without breaking a few eggs.
44. nest egg
45. to egg someone on
46. to have egg on one's face
47. a bad egg
48. cool as a cucumber
49. I'm going bananas.
50. play second banana
51. eat like a bird

continued

COOL AS A CUCUMBER, CONTINUED

52. just fell off the turnip truck
53. You can't squeeze blood from a turnip.
54. selling like hotcakes
55. living high on the hog
56. that takes the cake
57. a piece of cake
58. That's icing on the cake.
59. You can't have your cake and eat it, too.
60. eat like kings
61. I've got bigger fish to fry.
62. a fine kettle of fish
63. something smells fishy
64. packed like sardines
65. a red herring
66. my knees turned to jelly
67. so good it melts in your mouth
68. to make one's mouth water
69. Take it with a grain of salt.
70. worth his salt
71. rub salt in the wound
72. salt of the earth
73. to salt away
74. butter him up
75. bread and butter
76. sing for your supper
77. There's no such thing as a free lunch.
78. Life is a bowl of cherries.
79. to cherry pick
80. eating for two
81. born with a silver spoon in his mouth.
82. handed to you on a silver platter
83. like taking candy from a baby

84. not my cup of tea
85. either feast or famine
86. bring home the bacon
87. easy as pie
88. a sweet tooth
89. pie in the sky
90. in apple-pie order
91. to spill the beans
92. don't know beans about
93. not worth a hill of beans
94. full of beans
95. out to lunch
96. a couch potato
97. meat and potatoes
98. drop like a hot potato
99. small potatoes
100. crack a nut with a sledgehammer
101. in a nutshell
102. for peanuts
103. old chestnut
104. from soup to nuts
105. duck soup
106. souped up
107. in the soup
108. as thick as pea soup
109. use your noodle
110. chew the fat
111. cut the mustard
112. put some mustard on it
113. out of the frying pan and into the fire
114. half-baked idea
115. bear fruit
116. forbidden fruit
117. low-hanging fruit
118. fruit of one's labor
119. offer a carrot and stick
120. carrot top

121. cook up a storm
122. crème de la crème
123. to curry favor
124. glutton for punishment
125. stew in your own juices
126. to stew about something
127. in a pickle
128. One man's meat is another man's poison.
129. spice things up
130. recipe for disaster
131. salad days
132. score brownie points
133. square meal
134. upper crust
135. grist for the mill
136. to cook someone's goose
137. down the hatch
138. Your eyes are bigger than your stomach.
139. can't stomach it
140. eat and run
141. eat your heart out
142. eat your words
143. having a lot on your plate
144. sour grapes
145. whet your appetite

Why did the potato cross the road?

He saw a fork up ahead.

DICTIONARY STEW

 Use a dictionary to help you complete the items below.

1. Place the following words in the proper category below: *colander, coriander, cruet, citronella, chintz, carafe, cardamom, cinnamon, cumin, caraway, columbine.*

   Spices   Cooking Utensils   Other

2. Alphabetize the words in exercise #1.

3. What is the difference between *canapé* and *canopy, funnel* and *fennel, bouchée* and *bushel*? Use each pair in separate sentences.

4. Would you make tea from *belladonna* or *bergamot*? Why or why not?

5. Would you serve prosciutto to a vegetarian? Why or why not?

6. What does one do with *crudités*?

7. What is the difference between *bouillabaisse* and *bouillon*? Use both words in a sentence that demonstrates their meaning.

8. The following words have a food related meaning and a non-food meaning. Use each word twice in the same sentence, once with the food related meaning and once with the non-food meaning. (Example: You can **dip** into your allowance to pay for the **dip** for the party.)

   dash, dash
   dice, dice
   pinch, pinch

9. Which of the following words doesn't belong: *bisque, slumgullion, borscht, fricassee, burgoo, fondant.* Why?

10. The following list of "B" words are all processes used in cooking. Put the words in alphabetical order.

   braise, blanch, brew, barbecue, blend, blacken, beat, broil, boil, baste, bake

Did you know that there is no word in the English language that rhymes with *orange*?

Name _____

MORE DICTIONARY STEW

 Use a dictionary to help you complete the items below.

1. Use the words *baguette* and *briquette* correctly in the same sentence.

2. Use the words *cinnamon* and *cinnabar* correctly in the same sentence.

3. If someone says something is a *gustatory* delight, what do they mean?

4. If you *blanch* some almonds, what do you do to them?

5. Use *pasta* and *hosta* correctly in the same sentence.

6. Use the word *piquant* in a sentence about food.

7. Use the words *pullet*, *palette* and *palate* in a sentence about food.

8. In a sentence, *disparage* your least favorite food.

9. Rewrite this sentence so that it is easier to understand: *Each ramekin contained a copious quantity of succulent drupelets combined with julienned bananas and a dollop of cream.*

10. Alphabetize the following drinks:

*cocoa, soda, root beer, milk, juice, water, sparkling water, malt,
milk shake, tea, coffee, iced tea, lemonade, spritzer, tonic,
punch, java, espresso, cappuccino*

"Great
eaters and
great sleepers
are incapable of
anything else
that is great."

—Henry IV of France

Name _____

KEY INGREDIENTS

Every ingredient is important in a recipe. If the cook leaves something out, the results are often pretty strange. Imagine brownies without the chocolate, omelets without the eggs, or pizza without the crust.

Writing can also sound pretty strange if a key ingredient is left out. A sentence without a verb just doesn't work, for example. Neither does a sentence without a noun.

Some parts of speech *can* be left out. However, these parts of speech are so common in our language that leaving them out is actually hard to do. To show you how hard, follow the instructions below. Each answer should be *at least* three sentences long.

1. Write a description of your delicious meal last night at Food Heaven. Use no adjectives at all, except for the articles *a, an* and *the*.

2. Write a paragraph describing a parent and a child you saw eating at Food Heaven, but use no pronouns.

3. Write a description of a family eating dinner together in a booth at Food Heaven, but use no prepositions.

4. Write a description of what two servers did to try to please a demanding couple, but use no conjunctions.

"Strength is the capacity to break a chocolate bar into four pieces with your bare hands—and then eat just one of the pieces."

—Judith Viorst

COFFEE OR A ROLLER COASTER

s t r e t c h i n g   t h e   i m a g i n a t i o n

To encourage them to stretch their imaginations and exercise their creativity, try asking your students questions with no right or wrong answers. Any answer is acceptable, so long as students explain their reasoning.

Don't worry if *you* can't think of an answer to some of the questions. Often students will surprise you by coming up with answers you wouldn't have dreamed of in a million years. In fact, knowing that *you* can't think of an answer may encourage them to try even harder!

Example: Which is sadder, a cup of coffee or a roller coaster?
Answer: A cup of coffee is sadder. A roller coaster has its ups and downs, but coffee is always in a dark mood.

1. Which weighs less, a brownie or a smile?

2. What does broccoli have in common with a cell phone?

3. How is bread like a stapler?

4. Which is happier, a pepperoni pizza or a baseball cap?

5. Which is lonelier, a bowl of oatmeal or a hangnail?

6. Which is crazier, a salad or an eyebrow?

7. How is spaghetti like a motorcycle?

8. Which is funnier, a marshmallow or a fork?

9. Which is stronger, strawberry jelly or a butterfly?

10. What do an accordion and a tube of toothpaste have in common?

Name _____

CAFETERIA

PART A

There are many words hidden in the word *cafeteria*. Look for a food-related word that fits each definition below. For each answer, you may use only the letters in *cafeteria*. For each answer, you may also use each letter only as often as it appears in *cafeteria*.

1. Except for toddlers who play with their food, what most other people do at meal time: _____

2. A type of cheese made from goat's milk: _____

3. What the British drink with crumpets: _____

4. To serve food for special events, like weddings: _____

5. Something Jack Sprat could not eat: _____

6. Though some people gag at even the thought of it, many people love eating this part of a pig after pickling: _____

7. Where the French go for lunch: _____

8. A glass container used to serve coffee: _____

9. A side dish common with Mexican, Indian or Asian food: _____

10. A cooler isn't going to do you much good without this: _____

PART B

Now add 10 of your own definitions to this puzzle. You need not be limited to items with food-related answers, though. Your definitions can refer to *any* word that can be made from the letters in *cafeteria*.

Where do
baby cows eat
their lunch?

In a calf-eteria.

CHEESY RHYMES

Gilbert K. Chesterton, an early 20th century English writer, once said, "Poets have been mysteriously silent on the subject of cheese."

That is true. Most poets don't put cheese at the top of their list when it comes to topics for poems. James McIntyre (1827-1906), however, did. He wrote many poems about cheese. Sadly, they were *bad* poems, but poems nonetheless. Here's one stanza from his "Ode on the Mammoth Cheese":

> We have seen thee, queen of cheese,
> Lying quietly at your ease,
> Gently fanned by evening breeze,
> Thy fair form no flies dare seize.

 Now it's your turn. Write a rhyming poem about cheese, using any rhyme scheme you like.

Some cheese-related words and phrases to get you started thinking "cheesily":

cheddar	Muenster	Gouda
mold	fondue	Limburger
bleu cheese	Swiss	Parmesan
rind	American	cream
goat's milk	curds	cottage
ferment	Brie	
mozzarella	Edam	

 BONUS. For a bigger challenge, write a Shakespearean sonnet about cheese. The rhyme scheme for a Shakespearean sonnet is abab / cdcd / efef / gg.

What do you call cheese that belongs to someone else?

Nacho cheese.

OLIVIA'S CAFE

In the box below is a very detailed description of Olivia's Café. The problem is, it is *too* detailed. The details are thrown out randomly, with no rhyme or reason to their selection.

When describing something, it is a good idea to select details carefully to create a certain impression or to fill a certain purpose. For example, if you want to show that a classroom feels very serious and disciplined, you would *not* mention the jokes pinned up on the bulletin board. You *might* mention how all the students have their heads bent over their books and how all the rows are absolutely straight, with the shades adjusted to exactly the same height.

 Rewrite the description of Olivia's Café, below, choosing details that fill *one* of the following purposes:

- to show that Olivia's Café is a healthy, nutritious place to eat.
- to show that people will love the inviting, friendly atmosphere of Olivia's Café.

Feel free to rearrange or delete details in whatever way makes the most sense for your purpose.

Olivia's Café has cheerful yellow walls that invite people in. There is often a slight chlorine smell, but that is because of the staff's attention to cleanliness. There is a giant picture of Johnsonville painted on one wall. It shows every important building in town. The restaurant serves only whole grains. Smoothies are made with fresh fruit served in red tumblers decorated with rainbows. The owner, Olivia, has a cute dog name Henrikens, and she goes home every day at 1:00 to feed and pet him. She loves Henrikens more than about anything. All the sandwiches are made from whole grain breads and organic produce grown locally with no pesticides. Everything is artfully arranged and served on colorful red plates. The kitchen is stainless steel, and it sparkles. The health department gave the kitchen a "15," its highest mark for healthful practices. No trans fats are used in the cooking. The tables have white tablecloths and fresh flowers in the center. They are arranged in friendly little groupings. Sunshine streams through the windows. The owner of the hardware store next door usually parks his beat up Ford pick-up in front of the window. Special menus are available for diabetics or people with wheat allergies. People often sit and linger over coffee because it is so pleasant. Kids come in on dates. Ladies lunch there. The food is delicious. The servers wear cheerful red shirts in keeping with the red and yellow theme. Their shirts are always ironed and spotlessly clean. People love the smoothies, which are made with fresh fruit. If you are worried about kids having too much sugar, come here. Nothing has added sugar here; everything is sweetened naturally. No pizza is served here. Too bad! My favorite is sausage and mushroom, but my dad always wants to get ham and pineapple. Yuck! At least that's better than anchovy—the worst! We usually order our pizza from the Pepperoni Palace. It's right next door to Olivia's.

"Eating words has never given me indigestion."

—Winston Churchill

OVERSTUFFED SENTENCES

Have you ever tried to read something that was stuffed with big words? It was probably pretty hard to understand. Sometimes people mistakenly think that long, fancy-sounding words will make their writing sound more intelligent and important. Instead, their writing is just hard to understand.

Sometimes a big or unusual word is the best choice, but too many "polysyllabic" or obscure words can cloud the meaning of your writing. In general, simple is clearer.

POMPOUS AND UNCLEAR:

His gargantuan repast left him feeling distended and flatulent.

SIMPLE AND TO THE POINT:

His big meal left him bloated and gassy.

POMPOUS AND UNCLEAR:

Your culinary production is indubitably delectable.

SIMPLE AND TO THE POINT:

Your cooking is really delicious.

 Rewrite the sentences below so that they are simple, clear statements. You may use your dictionary to decode the long or obscure words.

1. The beef bourguignonne made my olfactory receptors twitch.
2. The vessel was laden with leguminous vegetables.
3. Most cuisine will be gustatorily enhanced with the supplementation of redolent allium.
4. She overindulged her ravenousness at the smorgasbord, resulting in emesis.
5. Although he wasn't rapacious, he gormandized five concave receptacles of an amalgamation of semolina and a liquid oxide of hydrogen.
6. You really comprehend how to prime victuals for consumption on the accessory heated by pieces of porous carbon or a gaseous fossil fuel.
7. I venerate any hominid who can concoct a satisfactory ambrosial molded form of a leavened composite.
8. Desist from being eminently fastidious regarding your provisions and endeavor to masticate unprecedented edible substances.
9. If I garnered a note of currency equaling one hundred of the most infinitesimal monetary units for every occasion someone queried me with, "Do you have a yearning to acquire fragments of a starchy tuber that have been submerged in scalding unctuous liquid to accompany your meal?", I'd be affluent.
10. Where's the confectionery that is customarily proffered at the cessation of ingesting the principal sustenance?

"Do not be tempted by a twenty-dollar word when there is a ten-center handy, ready, and able."

—William Strunk, Jr.

Name _____

IN COMMON...OR NOT

⊚ IN COMMON...

The following groups of foods are all linked together by something in common. Look at the food names and see if you can find the common denominator. (There may be more than one answer that fits.)

EXAMPLE:

bread, cherry pie, cookies, lasagna
What they have in common: all are cooked in an oven.

1. beef, strawberry, tomato, maraschino cherries_____

_____

2. ice cream, cereal, soup, pudding _____

_____

3. coffee, soup, mashed potatoes, pizza _____

_____

4. casserole, tossed salad, beef stew, trail mix _____

_____

5. cookie, hamburger, bagel, peppermint _____

_____

⊚ ...OR NOT

Now try a different twist. For each of the groups of foods below, figure out what all the items *except for one* have in common. In the space provided, write the item that doesn't belong and why it doesn't belong.

6. pudding, casserole, tortilla, beef _____

_____

7. potatoes, eggs, noodles, cake _____

_____

8. mango, banana, kiwi, pear _____

_____

"Eating rice cakes is like chewing on a foam coffee cup, only less filling."

—Dave Barry

BONUS. Add three items of your own to either section of this puzzle. Be sure to include an answer key.

SENTIMENTAL JOURNEY
s u m m a r i z i n g

Because people of all ages have memories in which food plays an important role, "food memories" can be an excellent basis for an exercise in collecting information and then summarizing it.

Ask students to choose an older adult to interview about his or her memories. Suggest that they choose someone older rather than younger, if they have a choice. Memories from older people will likely be very different from a student's own memories—and thus more interesting. (In the past 100 years, after all, food habits have changed tremendously. For example, people used to eat almost all their meals at home, or at the homes of friends. Now many people don't know how to cook at all, relying on microwave warm-ups and fast food.)

With your class, brainstorm a list of questions that students might ask. Here are a few ideas:

What kinds of food do you remember from your childhood days? What kind of candy was popular? What foods played a part in your family's traditions? Were any of the traditional foods in your family different from the foods of your friends and neighbors? Who did the cooking in your family? Was this person any good at it? Did you learn to cook at an early age? Or ever? Why or why not? Are there foods from your past that you miss? Don't miss?

Think about your years of dating. What kind of role did food play? Did you go out to eat? What were your favorite foods? Did you like to eat anything others thought was weird? Do you associate any food memories with a certain person? If so, who?

After you have brainstormed a long list of possible questions, have students select 10 questions for their interviews. Give some interview hints, such as choosing a time when the person has time to talk, letting him or her know what the assignment is, coming prepared with paper and possibly a tape recorder, being polite, etc.

Have students write one or two page summaries of what they have learned. Remind them that they need not write about everything they hear in their interview. Ask them to select what they find most interesting and what they think will be most interesting to others.

DELICIOUS AND DISGUSTING

◎ DELICIOUS

You stop. You stare. You drool. You have just caught sight of one of the most delicious foods on the planet. Describe this food, using details based on the five senses—sight, smell, touch, taste, hearing. However, do *not* reveal the name of the food or of any of the main foods that are used to create it.

For example, if you are describing meat loaf, you can't use the word "meat" or "hamburger." Instead, you must come up with a different way of saying "meat" or "hamburger." For example, you could say, "an animal product that is ground up." Instead of using the word "ketchup," you might say, "a thick goop made from something red and round that grows on vines."

When you are finished writing the description, trade papers with another student. Can your partner tell what food you are describing? Can you tell what he or she is describing? If so, you have done a fine job of using details to describe something without revealing directly what it is.

◎ DISGUSTING

You stop. You stare. You wince. You have just caught sight of one of the most disgusting foods on the planet. Just as you did with the delicious description (above), describe this food, using details based on the five senses—sight, smell, touch, taste, hearing. However, do *not* reveal the name of the food or of any of the foods that are used to create it.

Again, trade papers with a partner. Can you each tell what the other is describing?

DOUBLE TIME

Repeat both exercises above. If you did well the first time around, try to choose something even harder to describe. If you did not do well before, try to improve your descriptions this time.

"I do not like broccoli...
And I'm the president of the United States and I'm not going to eat more broccoli."

—George H.W. Bush

Name _____

APPETIZING ANTONYMS

When it comes to food, people have strong opinions. Mention brussels sprouts, and you will get a clear reaction from people: they either love them or hate them. There is generally no in-between. *Love* and *hate* are antonyms—word pairs that are opposite in meaning.

 Part A. Match each word on the left, below, to its *antonym* on the right.

1. good	a. lumpy
2. hot	b. tender
3. spicy	c. cold
4. crunchy	d. bland
5. raw	e. separate
6. sweet	f. weak
7. flavorful	g. dry
8. fresh	h. light
9. frozen	i. cool
10. wet	j. spoiled
11. blend	k. sour
12. thick	l. runny
13. crisp	m. cooked
14. smooth	n. creamy
15. solid	o. thawed
16. hard	p. tasteless
17. dark	q. liquid
18. strong	r. soggy
19. warm	s. bad
20. chewy	t. soft

 Part B. Use all of the pairs of antonyms, above, in sentences about food. You may write one sentence for each pair, or you can put more than one pair in the same sentence.

Note: Your sentences must make sense, and they must show the meaning of the words from the context. In other words, you can't write a sentence like, "*All these words are antonyms: up and down, in and out, white and black.......*"

What is invisible and smells like bananas?

Monkey burps.

Name _____

FOOD TO WRITE HOME ABOUT

People have strong feelings about various foods, and the feelings are very personal and unique to each individual. Use the questions and examples below to help you develop two short pieces (one to five paragraphs each) on foods that have very different effects on you.

 COMFORT FOODS. What is your comfort food? Even if we haven't thought about it, most of us have one. If you're sick, what food or beverage makes you feel better? If you've had a bad day, do you find yourself turning to a certain food? Does your mom or dad always serve tea and toast to anyone who is sick? Or 7-Up and crackers? Or...?

Everyone's comfort food is different. For Cheri, it's mashed potatoes. If she is feeling bad, she wants nothing but plain mashed potatoes with real butter on them. For Ian, it's Jell-O with bananas—and it's got to be orange Jell-O. Joe thinks anyone who is sick should have chicken soup, preferably made by his mother, no matter what the illness. When she has a cold, Elena wants spicy green chili to clear her sinuses because that's what Uncle Pedro always made for her when she was little.

Describe your comfort food. Why do you think it's a comfort to you? Describe a time you have turned to it for comfort.

FOODS THAT DO THE OPPOSITE. What food makes you gag? What food would you not even consider eating?

Maybe you came down with the stomach flu once after eating spaghetti, and now the thought of spaghetti makes you gag. Maybe poached eggs with their runny yolks make you sick because you find them disgusting to look at. Maybe it's peas because your mean babysitter made you eat peas and now you associate peas with her. Maybe your mother hates strawberries and taught you to hate them.

Describe what food (or foods) really disgust you, and why.

"As a child, my family's menu consisted of two choices: take it or leave it."

—Buddy Hackett

Name _____

REALISM SQUAD

You are part of the new Realism Squad in your state. The Realism Squad is a small but vocal group that thinks food descriptions have gotten out of hand. Restaurant menus make absolutely everything sound like a work of art. Descriptions on packaged food are completely unrealistic. Commercials make all food products sound wonderful.

Children are especially vulnerable. They hear that Chocolate Covered Caramel Toasted Sugar Loops make breakfast *fun*, and that's what they want their moms to buy. They see happy families eating at the Corner Chain Restaurant That Will Make Your Life Wonderful and Also Has a Trampoline and Video Games, and that's where they want to go.

As part of the Realism Squad, your job is to tone things down and to bring a strong dose of realism to food descriptions. Here are a couple of examples of the work you have done:

- A restaurant describes farm-fresh beef roasted in a demi-glace wine sauce. You change the description to this: *A hunk of muscle sliced from the side of a dead cow and stuck in the oven for three hours with a couple of cups of fermented grapes.*

- A commercial talks about the Corner Chain Restaurant's wonderful whipped potatoes, slathered in butter and served nestled next to delectable spears of organically grown asparagus. You change the description to this: *Some potatoes dug up from a garden where they were fertilized with manure and numerous pesticides, washed and boiled in unfiltered tap water until soft, then slathered in a by-product of cow's milk that was beaten until it solidified. All this is plunked on a plate next to some limp asparagus raised with only compost as fertilizer.*

 Now add a dose of realism to the following descriptions:

1. Our mouth-watering lunch speciality is chicken coated with golden bread crumbs, sauteed gently, and covered with crispy bacon and melted mozzarella cheese, all on sourdough bread. This delectable sandwich is served with a cup of creamy tomato soup made from a cherished family recipe handed down through the generations and made with Mom's tender loving care.

2. Even your family members with the heartiest appetites will leave Gargantuoso with smiles on their faces. At Gargantuoso, we believe that there's never too much of a good thing. Every dinner comes with mounds of perfectly cooked french fries, a never-empty jar of your favorite soft drink, and a sundae made with home-style brownies, creamy vanilla ice cream, and torrents of our special hot fudge sauce made with our special secret ingredient.

"Although I cannot lay an egg, I am a very good judge of omelettes."

—George Bernard Shaw

Name _____

DINNER CONVERSATION

Not every conversation goes the way we want it to. But here's your chance to have a conversation go *exactly* the way you want it.

 Write a one-page conversation that might take place over dinner. You get to choose the characters involved, the subject, the setting. You even get to put the words in their mouths!

Remember to punctuate your dialogue correctly. Put quotes around the words that the people actually say (not around the *he said/she said* dialogue tags). Change paragraphs each time you change speakers. For punctuation help, see the dialogue in the box below.

GETTING STARTED

Here are some questions to consider as you plan your conversation:

1. How many people are talking? Who are they?

2. What are they talking about?

3. Your conversation may be more interesting if a conflict or disagreement is involved. If there is a conflict or disagreement, what is it about?

4. What kind of personality does each person have? If a mother is involved, is she a gentle, coddling kind of mother, a strict, by-the-rules kind of mother, or...? If a child is involved, is he a studious little boy interested in bugs and dinosaurs? Or is he the kind of child likely to knock over things in the supermarket because of his rambunctiousness? Or...?

5. Where is the conversation taking place? At a restaurant? In the car? At home? On a picnic? At an amusement park? In the basement of a church?

"Food is an important part of a balanced diet."

—Fran Lebowitz

SAMPLE DIALOGUE

"What's for dessert?" asked Spencer. "I'm still hungry."

"Brussels sprouts pudding with whipped cream," said his mother.

Spencer sighed. "Do you think you're going to get tired of that vegetarian food cookbook pretty soon?"

"Not before I try the chocolate covered green beans with butterscotch tofu."

Name _____

IT'S ALL IN YOUR POINT OF VIEW

Everyone has encountered it—hearing people describe the same event in completely different ways. One person sees a movie and thinks it is the stupidest thing he has ever seen. Another person sees it and is moved to tears by its beauty. Still another is offended by its language. Another doesn't even notice its language at all.

How you view something may depend a lot on your point of view. A student may view a curfew as a terrible thing. A parent, however, may think of it as absolutely necessary. A policeman may look at a concert as dangerous, because of the number of people there. A teenager attending the concert may view it as exciting and thrilling.

Practice looking at things from the point of view of others. Describe a hamburger four different ways. Change your language, your opinions, and your words to fit the personality, as you imagine it, of each person. Write two or three sentences for each point of view.

1. Describe a hamburger from the point of view of a six-year-old dying to stop at McDonald's.

2. Describe a hamburger from the point of view of a vegetarian.

3. Describe a hamburger from the point of view of a father who has just grilled the perfect (in his mind) Fourth of July platter of burgers.

4. Describe a hamburger from the point of view of someone who works in a fast food restaurant and is really sick of it.

How can you tell if an elephant has been in your refrigerator?

Footprints in the Jell-O.

SUPER-SIZED FOOD CHALLENGE
f o l l o w i n g   d i r e c t i o n s

This game takes a bit of preparation, but it is great fun. It involves competition *between* groups, cooperation *within* groups, using research skills, and practice following directions carefully. It is a great game to use right before a vacation, for 1-3 class periods. It is noisy, but it is a productive kind of noise.

ORGANIZATION

Divide the class into groups of four. Students in each group should sit together, as far as possible from other groups.

Have each group create an official answer sheet. This can be a piece of notebook paper numbered from one to 75, with group members' names at the top. Some answers will require more than one line, so each group should have extra paper to staple to the official answer sheet when necessary.

Read aloud the first paragraph from "Super-Sized Instructions" (page 42). Then tell students that they are on their own. When they ask questions, insist that they read the instructions carefully and begin.

MATERIALS

*   Copies of the "Super-Sized Food Challenge" for each group.

*   Ordinary classroom reference materials, such as grammar books, literature books, dictionaries. Computers for each group are helpful, if available. It's also a good idea to bring in some extra materials, such as a set of encyclopedias, an almanac, and an atlas. Don't worry if all answers aren't available in your classroom. Students are to answer as many of the items as possible, not all of them. The challenge also relies on what they already know, as well as their ingenuity.

*   Tokens. Dried beans work great, but you can also use play money or poker chips. You will need a fairly large quantity of whatever you use.

SUPER-SIZED FOOD CHALLENGE, CONTINUED

SUGGESTIONS

*   Emphasize that the "Super-Sized Food Challenge" is an exercise in following instructions. Students will likely be confused at first, but keep referring them to the instructions. They will quickly catch on and realize that *they* must figure out what to do.

*   Allow students to have a negative balance of tokens by recording their balance on a tally you will keep. That's because students will almost certainly guess at answers in the beginning. When they go in the hole, they will learn to be more careful. (Note that incorrect answers lose *double* the designated number of tokens. Also, answers with misspelled words are considered incorrect.)

Name _____

SUPER-SIZED INSTRUCTIONS

This is an exercise in following directions, cooperating, and using your ingenuity. The purpose is to earn tokens by completing as many items as possible on the "Super-Sized Food Challenge" list you have received. The group with the most tokens at the end of the game will be the winner.

 Start by reading the instructions below.

- Be sure your group members' names are at the top of your official answer sheet.

- Be sure your official answer sheet is numbered from 1 to 75.

- Choose a designated "runner" for your group. Put a star or an asterisk beside the name of your runner on the official answer sheet.

- *Only* the designated runner can bring your official answer sheet to the teacher to be checked. All written answers must be on your official answer sheet.

- To complete the items on the "Super-Sized Food Challenge" list, you may use any resources in this room to help you—except for another group's answer sheet.

- You may complete the items in any order.

- Correctly completed items will be awarded the number of tokens specified in parentheses after each item. Incorrect answers will cause your group to lose *double* the specified number of tokens for that item.

- Each answer that is written must be legible and spelled correctly. Otherwise it will be considered incorrect. Be careful!!!

"If toast always lands butter-side down, and cats always land on their feet, what happens if you strap toast on the back of a cat and drop it?"

—Steven Wright

Name _____

SUPER-SIZED FOOD CHALLENGE

1. How many blackbirds are baked in a pie in the classic nursery rhyme, "Sing a Song of Sixpence"? (1)

2. What book contains the following statement: "The rule is jam tomorrow and jam yesterday, but never jam today"? (3)

3. On the website, www.nutria.com, there are recipes for "Heart Healthy Crock-Pot Nutria," "Nutria Chili," and "Nutria Ragondin Sausage Jambalaya," to name a few. What is nutria? (2)

4. True or false: If you go swimming less than one hour after eating, you will get cramps and drown. (1)

5. Robert Burns wrote a poem called "Address to a Haggis." What is a haggis? (2)

6. What is "roasting on an open fire" in the "The Christmas Song"? (1)

7. Which country uses the following spices: kesar, jaiphal, imli, lahsun? (2)

8. Is fugu dangerous? Why or why not? (3)

9. Wasabi is a member of the _____ family. (2)

10. Write down five adjectives that could be used to describe fajitas. (2)

11. What novel contains the following line: "Heaped up on the floor, to form a kind of throne, were turkeys, geese, game, poultry, brawn, great joints of meat, sucking-pigs, long wreaths of sausages, mince-pies, plum-puddings, barrels of oysters, red-hot chestnuts, cherry-cheeked apples, juicy oranges, luscious pears, immense twelfth-cakes, and seething bowls of punch, that made the chamber dim with their delicious steam"? (5)

12. How many tablespoons are in a cup? (3)

13. Write down 20 words that can be made with the letters in *chocolate*. (5)

14. What foods are mentioned in the song, "Take Me Out to the Ball Game"? (2)

15. Is *delicious* a noun, verb, adjective, or adverb in this sentence: *Harold made a delicious soup*? (3)

16. What cooking utensil was used as both a shield and a helmet by the armies of Genghis Khan? (4)

17. Write down 15 words that rhyme with *bread*. (4)

18. Use *their, they're,* and *there* correctly in one sentence about food. (2)

19. What was food writer Julia Child's astrological sign? (2)

20. Who invented potato chips? (2)

21. In what state is the Gilroy Garlic Festival held? (2)

22. Complete the following commercial jingle: "My _____ has a first name. It's _____." (1)

23. What does USDA stand for? (2)

What did the left eye say to the right eye?

Just between you and me, something smells!

Name _____

CHALLENGE LIST, CONTINUED

24. List five synonyms for the word *food*. (2)

25. Who is Beef Wellington named after? (2)

26. True or false: The Caesar salad was named after Julius Caesar. (2)

27. Write down 15 words that rhyme with *flax*. (4)

28. What is entomophagy? (3)

29. Write down the names of 10 edible flowers. (2)

30. Write down 10 bands named after food. (8)

31. What is jicama? (1)

32. Who wrote the memoir *Tender at the Bone?* What is its subtitle? (3)

33. *Tortilla Soup* is the name of a _____. (1)

34. What state is known as "America's Dairyland"? (1)

35. What famous chef wrote *The Art of French Cooking?* (1)

36. Write a *dependent clause* that mentions a food. (3)

37. Name a cartoon named after a legume. _____ (2)

38. Make up a 4-line rhyming song about any food, write it down, and come to the front of the room and sing it. The first team to do so will receive 25 tokens. Later groups will receive only 10.

39. What country is famous for its chocolate? (2)

40. What fruit is also a color? (1)

41. Name ten herbs. (3)

42. Complete this line from a well-known holiday song: Oh, bring us some figgy _____. (2)

43. What dessert is named after a famous horse race? (3)

44. Name ten berries. (2)

45. With Six You Get _____. (Hint: title of something) (3)

46. Name 10 clichés or common expressions that mention a food. (10)

47. Name ten food pairs—foods that are commonly mentioned together, such as *ham and eggs*. (4)

48. What is quince? (1)

49. What did Willy Wonka make in his factory? (1)

50. What is the origin of the expression, "Where's the beef?" (2)

51. Name two famous guys who make ice cream. (1)

CHALLENGE LIST, CONTINUED

52. What is a vegan? (1)

53. The one who earns money to feed the family is the _____ winner. (1)

54. Who was Popeye's girlfriend? (1)

55. Name five songs about food, or with a food in the title. (5)

56. What movie title mentions the jewelry store Tiffany's? (1)

57. Kids like to play a game called "Animal, _____, Mineral." (1)

58. Name five foods beginning with the letter *R* (2)

59. Write a sentence about any food, using at least 8 examples of *alliteration* in the sentence. (3)

60. What zodiac sign means "fish"? (1)

61. Name 10 foods that begin with the letter *C.* *(4)*

62. What is a *roux? (1)*

63. Which one of the following would a cook most likely put into a soup? *saffron* or *souffle* (1)

64. What is *feta* made of? (1)

65. What is *quinoa?* (1)

66. Little Miss Muffet ate curds and whey. What *are* curds and whey? (1)

67. We call them *cookies.* What do the British call them? (1)

68. Another name for *appetizers* has a very difficult spelling. This word is pronounced *or dervs.* How is it spelled? (2)

69. Who won the 1985 Orange Bowl? (2)

70. Only the first team to do this will win 8 tokens: Come to the front of the room and say, together, "For variety, we are going to sing a song that is *not* about food." Then sing "Itsy Bitsy Spider" and do the hand motions as you sing. (8)

71. Alphabetize these foods correctly: *spinach, salsa, Snickers, Snapple, sauce, Spam, soy sauce, salmon, soup.*

72. Complete this poem:

    I never saw a purple cow... (3) if you do one stanza, or (5) if you do two

73. Dr. Seuss wrote *Green Eggs and Ham.* Name 5 more books he wrote. (3)

74. *Personify* a potato in one sentence. (5)

75. Name 20 words that end in the letter *T.* At least ten of them must be foods. (4)

RACE OF TENS #1

 With your group, see how fast you can correctly complete each of the items below. In all your answers, do not mention the same food twice.

1. Name 10 vegetables.

2. Name 10 foods that end in "e."

3. Name 10 verbs that are used to describe food preparation.

4. Use each of the 10 verbs from #3 correctly in sentences.

5. Name 10 things a person might drink (nonalcoholic).

6. Name 10 foods that are red.

7. Name 10 foods that are round.

8. Name 10 foods that are six letters long.

9. Name 10 foods that are seven letters long.

10. Write a 10-word-long sentence about spaghetti.

"Personally,
I stay away from
natural foods. At my
age, I need all the
preservatives I can get."

—George Burns

Name _____

RACE OF TENS #2

 With your group, see how fast you can correctly complete each of the items below. You can't mention the same food twice.

1. Name 10 foods that are sour.

2. Name 10 fruits that grow on trees.

3. Name a food that starts with every *other* letter of the alphabet, starting with A. (The first item begins with A, the second with C, the third with E, etc.)

4. Use each word from #3 correctly in a sentence. (That will be a total of 13 sentences.)

5. How many words can you make from the words "Catsup and Mustard." Try for 10 X 10 (100!).

6. Alphabetize these ten foods correctly: *guava, granola, grape, grapefruit, gum, grain, ginger, gravy, gumbo, garlic.*

7. Name 10 spices.

8. Name 10 nouns.

9. Use each noun from #8 in a sentence that mentions food (one sentence for each noun).

10. Write a 10-word-long rhyming couplet about food. (A couplet is a rhyming poem of two lines.)

Nancy Astor:
"If you were my husband, Winston, I should flavour your coffee with poison."

Winston Churchill: "If I were your husband, madam, I should drink it."

Name _____

STORY STARTERS

 Choose one of the following as the start of a paragraph or short story:

1. Robert planted what he thought were carrot seeds in the backyard. Much to his surprise…

2. "The soup of the day is cream of termite," said the waitress…

3. It was a beautiful restaurant. It was a beautiful night. But then…

4. He took one bite, only one tiny bite…

5. The Estradas decided they never, ever should have thrown out Mrs. Campbell's fruitcake…

"Animals
are my
friends, and
I don't eat my
friends."

—George Bernard Shaw

Name _____

METAPHORS AND SIMILES

Similes and metaphors help make language interesting. If we say, "Henry was bald," we can certainly imagine Henry's head. But if we say, "Henry's head was as smooth and bare as a peeled, raw potato," we have a more interesting way of saying the same thing—with a simile. A simile is a comparison that uses the words "like" or "as."

A metaphor also uses a comparison, but without using the words "like" or "as." If Clarice says, "My life has been a roller coaster ride this month," she is comparing her life to a roller coaster ride. We can assume that it has had a lot of ups and downs, or perhaps that it has been very exciting.

 Use similes and metaphors related to food to describe three imaginary people. Each description should be only 1-3 sentences long, but it should create a vivid picture of the person.

EXAMPLE:

Neil's complexion was as pale as mashed potatoes, and his marshmallow middle puffed around his belt.

"Don't tell me
the moon is shining;
show me the glint
of light on broken glass."

—Anton Chekhov

Name _____

SATISFYINGLY SWEET AND SAVORY

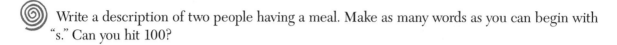 Write a description of two people having a meal. Make as many words as you can begin with "s." Can you hit 100?

One person started by writing, *Susan and Samantha slurped soup as they sat at Sid's Steakhouse one Saturday night.*

Another started with, *Susan and Sam stopped at SushiRama on Sunday, settled into soft satin pillows on the shiny floor, started studying the menu to select some starters, and finally settled on salmon.*

Scoring: Give yourself one point for every "s" word you use. Then have someone else score your paper. You will *lose* one point for every misspelled word, so be careful!

"Stressed spelled backwards is desserts. Coincidence? I think not!"

—Author Unknown

FOOD CHAIN

Normally, a food chain shows how living things get their food. Some animals eat plants and some animals eat other animals. However, no animal is going to devour another one in the kind of food chain you are going to create.

Choose a food, any food, to start your word chain. The last letter of that food should become the *first* letter of the next food. The last letter of that food will become the first letter of the next food, and so forth.

For example, if you start with the word "spinach," the next word could be "hamburger" because spinach ends in an "h" and hamburger begins with an "h." The next word could be "ravioli" because "hamburger ends in an "r" and "ravioli" starts with one. The word chain would look like this:

spinac<u>h</u>

<u>h</u>amburge<u>r</u>

<u>r</u>avioli

See if you can create a food chain at least 100 words long. Of course, it is important to make no spelling errors, as that can throw off your whole chain. Also, you can't name the same food twice.

"Mosquitoes remind us we are not as high up on the food chain as we think."

—Tom Wilson

Name _____

FOOD SCRAMBLE

 Below are fifty unrecognizable words. Your job? Unscramble the letters in each item to spell a common food.

1. rgemrhbua
2. unctooc
3. ganaasl
4. noolevopr
5. hacnpsi
6. azpzi
7. logceamau
8. nacnoinm
9. kcnaeaps
10. hasqsu
11. tgdhoo (two words)
12. linkcemuppre
13. saagpursa
14. lfawesf
15. cioblorc
16. naaban
17. bripeimr (2 words)
18. oancb
19. rekhcoiat
20. thapeisgt
21. eerppnoip
22. noeltpacau
23. amlwlmhrsoa
24. iuhss
25. dooacva

26. oesslerca
27. mooatt
28. eolnmtrawe
29. lopteboorl
30. urossetlsuspbsr (2 words)
31. omosurhm
32. laeqdlaius
33. aoanmcir
34. guessaa
35. aneneresgb (2 words)
36. pkoohcpr (2 words)
37. ofaltema (2 words)
38. soetpaot
39. ablemltas
40. eaorcdbnr (2 words)
41. littlenoir
42. kayierit
43. aplegtng
44. turbroi
45. aappay
46. gamon
47. dilchaaen
48. oledeanm
49. aegbl
50. iehnckc

Where do ants go
for a vacation?

Frants.

Name _____

SOMETHING FISHY'S GOING ON

Puns. People love them. People hate them. People laugh when they hear them. People groan when they hear them.

Love them or hate them, human beings can't seem to help themselves. They create puns all the time, accidentally and on purpose.

What exactly *is* a pun? It is a humorous play on words, often involving double meanings. People making fish puns might mention an opporTUNAty. Or they might describe something as FIN-tastic.

 Write a *punny* story full of fish puns. You can make up your own puns or borrow some of the puns below. See if you can include at least 10 fish-related puns in your story.

- What's all this I keep *herring* about…
- Don't *flounder* around.
- getting *crabby*
- *Exsalmon* (examine) it.
- That's a *moray!* (That's amore!)
- Put some *mussel* behind it…
- *perch*ed on a chair
- stop *carp*ing
- *clam* up
- super-*fish*-al (superficial)
- got *reeled* in
- Don't *shell* out too much
- a-*fish*-ionado (aficionado)
- having a *whale* of a time
- *fish*ing for compliments
- something *fishy* going on
- my hands are *clam*my
- heart and *sole* (soul)
- You're so *shellfish*! (selfish)

What do you call a fish with no eyes?

FSH.

Name _____

SENTENCE COMBINING

Newspapers are known for using fairly short, simple, straightforward sentences. But imagine that a newspaper takes this short sentence business a bit too far with a piece like this:

There was a fire. The fire was yesterday. It was at a restaurant. The restaurant was Spaghetti Land. The restaurant was popular. Spaghetti Land is located on 5th Street. The restaurant was destroyed. It was a fire that destroyed it. The restaurant is next to another restaurant. That restaurant is Antonio's Taco Factory. The fire also damaged Antonio's Taco Factory. The damage was estimated at around $100,000.

This writing could certainly be improved by combining the information into fewer sentences. There are many ways the sentences could be combined. Here are three ideas:

Yesterday, a fire destroyed the popular Spaghetti Land restaurant on 5th Street. The fire also did about $100,000 damage to the next-door restaurant, Antonio's Taco Factory.

The popular Spaghetti Land restaurant on 5th Street was destroyed yesterday by a fire that also damaged Antonio's Taco Factory next door. Damage to Antonio's was estimated at around $100,000.

A fire was responsible yesterday for destroying one popular local restaurant and damaging another. The Spaghetti Land restaurant on 5th Street was destroyed, and Antonio's Taco Factory next door sustained around $100,000 in damage.

Here are two more stories that go overboard with short sentences. Rewrite each story at least *two* different ways. Be sure not to leave out any information. Try to use no more than four or five sentences in each rewrite.

1. *Victor was hungry. His hunger was extreme. His hunger occurred at lunchtime. He went to the cafeteria. The cafeteria was in his school. He looked at the food. The food was being scooped onto trays. It was kind of brownish. It resembled meat. He wasn't sure it was meat. He wasn't sure it was food. He was sure of one thing. It did not look good. He did not want any. He had a granola bar. It was in his backpack. It was squashed. It would probably taste better than the brownish food.*

What did
the cannibal
have for lunch?

Baked beings.

2. *Allie was babysitting Tyrone. Tyrone has a nickname. The nickname is Terrible Tyrone. Tyrone is two. Allie was trying to feed him peas. Tyrone doesn't like peas. He doesn't like babysitters. He spit the peas. He spit them clear across the room. Some of them landed in other places. One of those places was Allie's hair. Allie was mad. She had a date later. The date was with Calvin. She really likes Calvin. She doesn't like Tyrone very much. She also doesn't like something else. That something else is peas in her hair.*

Name _____

DISHING UP THE INTERNET

Dictionaries are great. However, they don't have everything. For some things, the Internet is more helpful for quick answers. Use Internet search engines and an online dictionary to answer the following:

1. Look at the three words below. One is found in a garden, one is found in the ocean, and one is found in the desert. Which is which?

   aubergine_____

   abalone_____

   agave_____

2. What do the following words all have in common: *zeppola, beignet, fritter?*

3. Which part of a cow does *flank steak* come from: *shoulder, rib, front, back, head, belly, foot?*

4. Name two things wrong with this sentence: Senora Morales was eating in the Mexican cottage where she grew up. She cut open the jambon and spooned out the strawberry jam inside of it. "This jambon is delicious. It must have come from a happy cow," said her father.

5. What is the main ingredient in *p'tcha?*

6. Write one sentence that uses all of the following words correctly: *ganache, garnish, garbure.*
   _____

7. Which word doesn't belong in the following list: *vichyssoise, cioppino, pappardelle, borscht, gazpacho, bouillabaisse.*

8. What famous cook and food writer said, "You don't have to cook fancy or complicated masterpieces—just good food from fresh ingredients." _____.
   Name one book that this person wrote. _____

9. How do *quick breads* differ from regular breads? _____
   _____

10. What, exactly, is lard? _____
    What nonedible item that most of us use every day is made from lard? _____

"Never eat more than you can lift."

—Miss Piggy

Name _____

WHERE'S THE FOOD?

Can you find the foods hidden in the sentences below? The letters are in the correct order, but they are sometimes spread out over more than one word. There are two foods hidden in each sentence. Underline or highlight the letters that spell the food.

EXAMPLE

Mom bough**t ea**ch of the children a cookie but made Bian**ca ke**ep hers until her homework was finished.

1. I'm impressed that Bob read the entire book to Benjamin.

2. Meet me at 10:00 in front of the train depot at Oesterfield and 42nd Avenue.

3. I asked the rich American tourist if she could maybe answer my question.

4. I hope a chestnut tree will grow in my one acre, amazingly beautiful garden.

5. George went to a street dance, but Terry decided to go to the library.

SUPER CHALLENGE

Add one to five sentences to this puzzle, hiding at least five more food words. (You can put all of the words in one sentence, if you can. Or you can spread them out over one to five sentences.)

Of course, spelling is *very* important in a puzzle like this!

**Recipe for
Elephant Stew**

1 Elephant, Medium size,
2 rabbits (optional), gravy.

Cut elephant into bite size pieces and
cover with gravy. Cook over kerosene fire for
about 4 weeks at 465 degrees F. This elephant serves
3,800 adults and 35 children. If more are expected, two
rabbits may be added. Do this only if absolutely necessary,
as most people do not like to find a hare in their stew.

Name _____

YOU ARE HOW YOU EAT

You have probably heard the common phrase, "You are what you eat." In this activity, think, "You are *how* you eat."

Write a paragraph that describes someone eating and, at the same time, lets the reader know something important about that person—but without actually saying outright what it is that is important.

For example, perhaps you want to indicate that the person is very tense. Don't write, "This person is tense." Instead, show that she is tense. Describe her nervous gestures as she slurps her soup: her glances left and right, her rigid shoulders, her shaky hands, etc. Let readers figure out on their own that the person is tense.

Some ideas to think about for your description:

- Who is the person you are describing?

- Is the person upset? Happy? Tense? Excited? Bored? Or...?

- Is the person a strong leader? A great coach? Extremely smart? Very athletic? Suspicious? Mean? Kind? Or...?

- Where is the person eating?

- Is anyone eating with the person?

- Is there a server serving this person? If so, how does the person eating treat the server?

Choose your words carefully to portray something important about the person eating, but without stating it outright.

Why don't cannibals eat clowns?

Because they taste funny.

Name _____

VERBING YOUR FOOD

The 25 words in the box below can be used to express actions involving foods. In other words, these food-related words can all be used as verbs.

bake	serve	grill	microwave
oil	slurp	stir	freeze
slice	heat	mix	chill
chop	blend	grate	thaw
dice	chew	roll	flour
peel	gulp	boil	season
beat	sip	roast	melt
burn	salt	scramble	drink

Interestingly, these words are not *necessarily* verbs. In the English language, it depends on how they are used. For example, look at the word *salt* in the following sentences:

Will you please *salt* that meat before you grill it?
He poured *salt* on his eggs.

In the first sentence, salt is indeed a verb. It shows action. In the second sentence, though, *salt* is a noun. It does not express the action in the sentence. That is expressed by *poured*.

The words in the box above can be used as nouns *or* verbs. Choose 10 of them. For each, write a sentence using the word as a verb and another sentence using the word as a noun. (Or, for a bigger challenge, try using some of the words as a noun and as a verb in the same sentence!) You can change the form of any of the words—*grilled, grilling, grills,* etc.

What does the richest person in the world make for dinner every night?

Reservations.

Name _____

ALEX HATED IT

How many ways can you find to say, "Alex hated it," without saying "Alex hated it"? (What Alex hated is a certain food.) Write at least 10 sentences.

1. _____
2. _____
3. _____
4. _____
5. _____
6. _____
7. _____
8. _____
9. _____
10. _____

How many ways can you find to say, "Alex served it," without saying "Alex served it." Try to create a different picture with each sentence, but don't forget to keep the meaning, "Alex served it."

1. _____
2. _____
3. _____
4. _____
5. _____
6. _____
7. _____
8. _____
9. _____
10. _____

The most remarkable thing about my mother is that for thirty years she served the family nothing but leftovers. The original meal has never been found."

—Calvin Trillin

Name _____

YOU ARE WHAT YOU EAT

Transitional expressions, or transitions, help to move readers along smoothly when they read. Without transitions, the writing can sound robotic, like this:

I woke up early. I took a shower. I ate breakfast. I watched television. I argued with my sister. She wanted to eat the last bagel. I grabbed it. I waited for the bus. I fell asleep. I missed the bus.

Transitions help to make the writing flow:

I woke up early and took a shower. Then I ate breakfast while I watched television. I argued with my sister because she wanted to eat the last bagel, but I managed to grab it. Afterward, I waited for the bus. Unfortunately, I fell asleep and missed it.

COMMON TRANSITIONS

first • although • after • afterward • also • and • before • besides • but • or
eventually • finally • yet • second • third • however • meanwhile • yesterday
on the other hand • next • similarly • since • then • therefore • today • unless
until • while • initially • because • furthermore • later • suddenly • nevertheless

---

 The story below has no transitions and, therefore, does not read smoothly. It sounds rather choppy and disjointed. Add transitions to make it read more smoothly.

You Are What You Eat

Allison woke up. She knew something was wrong. She had always heard the saying, "You are what you eat." She wasn't prepared for this. Next, she whipped back her covers. She stared down at herself in shock. Yesterday she had been a normal girl. Today she was a slice of pepperoni pizza. She couldn't believe her eyes. True, her mother had warned her. She had told her that she should eat healthier food. She had not paid attention. Now that she was an actual slice of pizza, she could see how fattening she was. She could see how greasy she was. She really did smell good. "I'm making myself hungry," she thought.

She heard her mom calling her down to breakfast. "Hurry up. You'll be late for school!" Allison panicked. What was she supposed to wear to school? She didn't have any clothes that would fit over pepperoni and cheese.

Allison's little brother, Leo, was struggling to open his bedroom door. He had been transformed into an ice cream cone. He was melting, fast.

"This recipe is certainly silly. It says to separate two eggs, but it doesn't say how far to separate them."

—Gracie Allen

THE FOOD BATTLE

Now that you have had some experience finding and recognizing transitions, try adding them to a story to make it hold together better.

The story that follows has no transitions and, therefore, does not read smoothly. It sounds a bit choppy and disjointed. Add transitions to make it read more smoothly. (Many commonly used transitions are listed in the box, below.)

COMMON TRANSITIONS

first • although • after • afterward • also • and • so • before • besides • but
eventually • finally • yet • second • third • however • meanwhile • yesterday
on the other hand • next • similarly • since • then • therefore • today • unless
until • while • initially • because • furthermore • later • suddenly • nevertheless

---

Alexander hated oatmeal. He really, really, really hated oatmeal. He hated it so much he absolutely refused to eat it.

Alexander's mother thought oatmeal was very, very, very good for a child. She made it every morning for Alexander. Every morning there was a battle. Alexander whined. He pouted. He cried. He tried feeding the oatmeal to the cat when his mother wasn't looking. He tried feeding it to his sister, who was only a baby and didn't understand how awful oatmeal tastes.

Once he even slipped some oatmeal into his shoes. He walked with squishy feet to the bathroom and scraped the oatmeal into the toilet. He flushed it down. He didn't notice that oatmeal had squished out over the top of his shoes and left little drops all the way from the kitchen to the bathroom.

His mother was on the lookout for oatmeal tricks. She watched Alexander like a hawk every morning. Alexander gave up. Every morning he sighed, held his nose, and choked it down. He felt full then. He felt sick.

His mother felt happy.

"Part of
the secret of
success in life is
to eat what you like
and let the food fight it
out inside."

—Mark Twain

Name _____

ADDING SOME ORDER

Aunt Fritzi is trying to tell you how to make potato soup. However, Aunt Fritzi tends to be a bit scatterbrained and doesn't exactly give straightforward directions. She also doesn't use many transition words.

Below are Aunt Fritzi's directions for making potato soup. Rearrange her words and rewrite as necessary so that you have clear, organized instructions. Feel free to cut anything that is unnecessary. Add transition words to make the directions clearer.

I'm so glad you want to know how to make my potato soup! Before I forget, remember not to cook it too long. Don't simmer it for more than 10 minutes after you add the milk, or the potatoes will get too soft. Start with a medium onion. Chop it up really, really fine. Your Uncle Harvey loves onions, so sometimes I put more in. You could, too. It's up to you. If you don't have about four cups of milk, be sure to run to the store before you get to the part where you add potatoes. I've done that—chopped up the onions and potatoes and then found out I didn't have enough milk. Be sure you have some. Anyway, after you chop up the onions, peel about four potatoes. If you don't mind potato soup with peelings in it, leave them on. It's easier that way. I like potato peelings. So does your Uncle Harvey. I usually leave them on. When company comes, I usually peel them. Some people just can't stand potato peelings. I don't understand it, but there you are. If you don't peel them, wash them really well. Whether you peel them or not, cut them into real small pieces. Put the potatoes in a pan and just barely cover them with water. Cook them until they just start to get soft—about 15 minutes, usually. Drain them really well. You know what's really great with potato soup? Homemade corn bread! Some people like to add a little sour cream and some bacon bits to each bowl of soup when it's served. It tastes great, but it is *so* fattening. Drain the potatoes. Go back to the onions. Melt a little butter in a big pan. Add the onions. Cook them until they are soft. Add the drained potatoes. Add some milk—about four cups. Maybe five. Heat the milk and potatoes gently until everything is piping hot. If you like your soup to be thick, put a couple of tablespoons of flour in a cup. Stir in about half a cup of cold water and mix until smooth. Add this to the soup. It will thicken it up. Oh yes, add salt and pepper to the potatoes when you add the milk. Choose red potatoes for this soup. They really work the best. Don't use sweet potatoes. They wouldn't work at all. This is an easy, fast meal.

Why do cows use MP3 players?

For moosic.

Name _____

AUDIENCE, AUDIENCE, AUDIENCE

One of the most important things to remember when you are writing is this:

Who is your audience?

It is important to put yourself in the reader's shoes and try to use language, terms, and an attitude that your audience will understand.

For example, if you are writing an e-mail to a close friend, it's fine to use a very casual approach with slang and maybe even abbreviations common in text messaging. If you are writing an essay for a college application, though, you will want to use a different approach, at least if you want to be taken seriously.

Write one short paragraph about an imaginary (or real!) visit to a restaurant and something strange or interesting that happened there—but write it three different ways, according to your audience. Make each description appropriate for the intended audience.

1. Your audience is a good friend of yours, and you are writing an e-mail.

2. Your audience is the manager of the restaurant, and you are writing a letter.

4. Your audience is your great-grandmother, and you are putting a note in a greeting card.

"Life expectancy would grow by leaps and bounds if green vegetables smelled as good as bacon."

—Doug Larson

ALPHABETICALLY SPEAKING

Write a story exactly 26 sentences long. The subject of the story can be anything related to *food*. Here's the hard part: The first sentence must begin with "a," the second with "b," the third with "c," and so on through the alphabet. (For *x* you may cheat and use a word beginning with the prefix *ex.*)

Here's an example of how a story might start:

> **A** *customer walked into Joe Schmoe's Dinner Delight at 11:00 p.m.* **B***ecause he was closing up, Joe didn't want to serve the customer.* "**C***rispy fried chicken, mashed potatoes, green beans, rolls, and cherry pie," said the customer.*
>
> "**D***on't you see the CLOSED sign I'm putting in the window?"*
>
> "**E***ating is what I want to do, and I'm going to do it now," said the man, plopping on a stool at the counter.*
>
> "**F***rustrated, Joe stood in the front of the customer and spoke slowly.* "**G***o away!" he said.*

Teacher: Give me a sentence that starts with the letter "I."

Jane: I is ...

Teacher: No, you don't say, "I is." You say, "I am."

Jane: Okay, I am the ninth letter of the alphabet.

Name _____

VERBING

People like to know what is *happening*. That's why verbs are so important. They are the action. They have power. Take a look at how a simple verb can completely change the meaning of a sentence:

Little Anthony **adored** clowns.
Little Anthony **despised** clowns.
Little Anthony **tripped** clowns.
Little Anthony **worshipped** clowns.
Little Anthony **collected** clowns.

 See how many ways you can change the sentences below by simply replacing the verb in each. Use at least five different verb replacements for each sentence:

1. Fluffikins **drank** the milk.

2. Ashley **drove** the ice cream truck.

3. Elwood **invited** his personal chef.

4. Grandmother **cooked** the meat loaf.

5. Someone **stole** the turkey.

Why did the
tomato blush?

It was embarrassed
to see the salad dressing.

FORESHADOWING
d i s c u s s i o n

Talk with students about how we are all familiar with *foreshadowing*, whether we realize it or not. It's everywhere—in movies and television shows, plays, short stories and books. For an example, you might use Juliet's lines from the balcony scene in *Romeo and Juliet*. Looking down at him, she says:

> Methinks I see thee, now thou art below,
> As one dead in the bottom of a tomb:
> Either my eyesight fails, or thou look'st pale.
> O God, I have an ill-divining soul!

Of course, this foreshadows Romeo's death at the end of the play. The lines give a hint of what is to come. A couple of other examples:

- A family moves into a new vacation house deep in the woods, and the mom, dad, and three children sit around the fireplace toasting marshmallows and having so much fun...and then the father looks outside later and pauses, seeing a pair of eyes among the trees. "It must be a deer," he thinks.

  Of course, it's not a deer. The mention of the eyes is foreshadowing, a hint that something dangerous lurks in those woods.

- A guest is staying with a family for Thanksgiving. They don't know her well, but she's a friend of Uncle Edwin's. She seems delightful. She is so funny. She helps with the dishes. She plays Monompoly with the kids. And then, when the son gets up to go to the bathroom, he sees a light in the den. He walks over and sees the guest opening a drawer in the den.

  This event foreshadows something dishonest the guest is going to do.

Have students get into small groups and first see if they can think of three examples of foreshadowing from television shows or movies they have seen, or short stories or books they have read. Everyone in the group need not have seen the movie or read the same book. Simply have group members prepare to share their examples with the class.

The exercise simply helps students become more aware of foreshadowing. A nice follow up is "Red Herrings," page 67, as many examples of foreshadowing do turn out to be red herrings.

RED HERRINGS

A red herring is not a fish. Well, it *can* be a fish, but it is often a term used to describe something designed to throw us off track. For example, imagine that you are reading a mystery called *The Murder of the Gourmet Chef*. A detective is trying to determine who stabbed the chef, and she is investigating all leads. She finds out that the chef and his brother had an argument the day before the murder. She goes to question him, and she sees the brother's sword collection hanging on a wall.

So...you suspect that the brother murdered the chef, right? You are wrong. In the end, it turns out that the murderer was the restaurant hostess. The sword collection was a *red herring*—a clue or piece of information that turns out not to have anything to do with the story line at all.

Why is a fact that turns out to be irrelevant called a red herring? Some believe it comes from fox hunting. In order to save a fox, a person could drag a strong-smelling red herring across the trail, thus confusing the dogs. (Others say this is ridiculous. Who would have been the one dragging the herring and wanting to save the fox?) Others believe British fugitives rubbed herring across their trail to divert bloodhounds pursuing them. Others say that poachers used the scent of herring to throw dogs off the trail of game. In any case, when you hear about a *red herring* today, it is referring to something that is distracting and turns out to be irrelevant.

 Pick out the *red herring* in each paragraph below.

1. In the *Adventures of Milhouse,* Milhouse's mother can't find him one day after school. She does find his notebook, and she finds a note about meeting "D" at Henry's coffee shop at 5:00. There has just been a warning in the paper about the coffee shop bandit targeting kids, so she calls the police. They go to the coffee shop and there is Milhouse. He is with his dad, who wanted to see his son before leaving town on a business trip but had forgotten to check with his ex-wife (Milhouse's mother) first. She had forgotten to check messages and didn't hear that Milhouse had told her where he would be.

2. A new tax to improve the library is not a good idea. We can't afford the tax as many people in this community recently lost their jobs when the big Florn Plant closed. The new tax would be a hardship on so many people. The current supply of books is perfectly usable. The current computers still work just fine. But mainly, it is not a good idea because the head librarian insists on keeping that awful book, *Bad Stuff*, on the shelves. It isn't right.

3. Ladies and gentlemen of the jury, let's look at the facts. The defendant was at the scene of the murder. His fingerprints are on the murder weapon. His mother is also in prison for murder, and is serving her 25th year of a 55-year sentence. He had a motive for the murder—the victim had fired him the day before. And, finally, a witness saw him holding an ax.

What sits at the bottom of the sea and shivers?

A nervous wreck.

GOLDILOCKS FOR THE 21ST CENTURY

The fairy tale "Goldilocks and the Three Bears" has been updated for the 21st century. The problem is that the update is full of spelling errors—101 of them, to be exact. Find and correct all 101 errors.

Once apon a time, a gril named Goldilocks decided to go four a run on the trial in the forest nere the development wear she lived. She put on her running shoes and grabbed her mp3 player and was off, listening to her favrite toons.

After she had been running for about fourty-five minuts, she was suprised to see a little cottage nessled in the woods. She did'nt know that three bears lived in the cotage—a mama bear, a papa bear, and a baby bear.

Curius, she desided to investagate. She walked up to the cottage and peaked in. No one seemed to be around, but she saw there were three bowls of food sitting on the tabel. Goldilocks was hungry and decided to clime in the window. Sometimes she did'nt make the wizest choices.

She lookt at the bowels. "Hmmmm," she said. "It seems to be poridge. I've never tasted poridge before. But I am hungry, so I'll try it." She took a spoonfull frum the papa bear's bowel. "This is to hot." She took a spoonfull from the mama bear's bowl. "This is too cold." She took a spoonfull from the baby bear's bowel. "This is just right!" she said. "But it tastes awful!" She swallowed hard and tride not to through up.

Then she saw three chairs. She was tiered from running and decsded to rest. She sat in the papa bear's chair. It was too hard. She set in the mama bear's chair. It was two soft. She sat in the baby bear's chair. It was just right! Unfortunitely, Goldilocks was heavier then the baby bear, and the chair broke. "Oops," said Goldilocks. She really was an iresponsible girl some times. She shruged her sholders and went into the bedroom, were she saw three beds.

She tried the papa bear's bed and the mama bear's bed and found them, just as you might ecpect, too hard and too soft. "This is quiet fustrating," she said. Then she snugled into the baby bear's bed. "Ahhh.....just right!" she smiled. She tenced up for a moment, worying that the bed mite brake. It didn't. She relacksed and fell fast asleep.

In just a little while, the three bears came back from *their* run in the woulds.

"I'm tired!" said the baby bear. "I'm starrving, too."

Name _____

GOLDILOCKS, CONTINUED

"I'm tired of listning to you complain," said Papa Bear. "Sit down and eat you're porridge."

"I want Frosted Choclate Oat Yummies!" said Baby Bear. "Nobody eats porridge anymore!"

"You due," said Mama Bear. "Now hush and take a byte."

Baby Bear looked arownd for some kind of distraction. He was *not* going to eat porridge, no madder what. He was thrilled to see that his littel chair was broken. He pertended to be upset, but he really wasnt. He thot it was time he got a lether recliner.

"My chair!" cried Baby Bear. "Somone broke it!"

"Is that someone *you*?" asked Papa Bear suspisiously.

"Wood I lye?" Baby Bear put on his most inosent face.

Papa Bear frowned. "I do remember the incident involving the cat and the choclate puding...," he started.

"Never mind that, Dad," said Baby Bear. "You look tired. I think its time we all took a nap."

Papa Bear looked suspicious, but he *was* tired. He agreed, and they all went itno the bedroom.

"There's a gril in my bed!" cryed Baby Bear.

"What did I tell you about lying?" yelled Papa Bear.

"Know, really! Look!"

All three bears crouded around Goldilocks. Just than, she woke up.

"This bad dream seems very reel," she murmerred, rubing her eyes.

Papa Bear grouled.

"Clam down, deer," said Mama Bear.

Papa Bear grouled again.

Goldilocks relized that she was knot in a dream. "Ummmmm, I think I'll be going," she said, siting up.

Papa Bear grouled again, very lowdly.

Goldilocks was glad she had'nt taken off her runing shoes. She leeped out of bed and ran out of that house as fast as she could.

Papa Bear turned to go after her, but Mama Bear grabbd his arm. "Let her go, deer," she said. "You don't need her. We still have all that nice poridge too eat."

What do you get if you cross a skunk with a bear?

Winnie the Pooh.

APOSTROPHE-ITIS

Restaurants are often guilty of apostrophe-itis or quotation mark-itis. In other words, someone writing the menus or the signs for the restaurant goes a little nuts with apostrophes and/or quotation marks and uses them inappropriately.

Here are the only times apostrophes should be used:

- To show that letters have been left out, as in *wouldn't* (*would not* with the "o" left out).
- To show that something "belongs" to someone, as in *Casey's smile* or *Bart's father Homer.*

Generally, there are only three times when quotation marks should be used:

- To note someone's exact words. (Sherianne said, "I do not like green eggs and ham.")
- To show that something doesn't quite mean what the words say it means. For example, look at the second item about apostrophes, above. The word "belongs" is in quotation marks. That's because of the example used. We don't usually think of a father as "belonging" to a boy. The quotation marks show that the word is used in a special sense. Quotation marks should be used sparingly for this purpose.
- To show that a title is the name of a song, short story, or other fairly short item.

That's it. Now, using that information, correct each of the items from restaurant signs and menus, below.

1. Special for the day: spinach omelets with "cheddar" cheese

2. Satisfaction is "guaranteed." We want all customer's to leave the Phish Pharm happy.

3. Sign in the kitchen: Each waiter's apron must be clean. Each waiter must wash hands after leaving the "rest room." Each waiters pants must be black. Mrs. Gomez says, "Any waiter whose shirt is not sparkling white and freshly ironed will be sent home to change."

4. The chicken is grilled and served on a bed of romaine lettuce leave's, with our signature lemon and artichoke dressing on the side. Waiters sing That's Amoré while you eat.

5. We believe that the customer who isnt satisfied is a customer who deserves better. At Penelope's Pie Palace we do our "best" to please everyone.

6. Each persons order is treated with the utmost in care. Our chef says, We want you to come back again and again.

7. Chef Anthonys creations are the talk of the town.

8. Weve got pie's, cookie's, doughnut's, cake's, and other goodies that will make your mouth "water."

A man went to the doctor with a carrot in one ear and a banana in the other. "What's wrong with me?" he asked.

The doctor replied, "You're not eating properly."

Name _____

DAILY BREAD

For each category listed along the side of the page, think of an appropriate word that begins with the letter at the top of the page. The first item is done for you.

	B	R	E	A	D
Desserts	blueberry pie				
Vegetables					
Verbs related to cooking or eating					
Six-letter food names					
Things people normally use in sandwiches					
Three-syllable food names					
Words that might describe a food					

"If you have two loaves of bread, sell one and buy a lily."

—Chinese proverb

JELL-O SCULPTURE CONTEST

⊙ Below are some useful words to know—even the rather weird sounding ones. Using a dictionary for help, match the words on the left with the definitions on the right.

_____ 1. magnanimous	a. a loud burst of laughter
_____ 2. guffaw	b. high-minded, noble, generous
_____ 3. mollycoddled	c. astonished
_____ 4. flabbergasted	d. in a haphazard manner
_____ 5. willy-nilly	e. to trick or deceive by underhanded methods
_____ 6. flippant	f. a silly, scatterbrained person
_____ 7. lollygagging	g. to pamper or overprotect
_____ 8. flibbertigibbet	h. to waste time, dawdle
_____ 9. inconsolable	i. disrespectful, not serious
_____ 10. bamboozle	j. brokenhearted

⊙ Read the story that follows and fill in the blanks with the appropriate words (or form of the words) from the list above. One word is used twice, the rest of them only once.

Nancy raced out of her apartment and down the sidewalk, running (1) _____

around pedestrians as she tried to hale a cab. There would be no (2)_____

on this particular day. She was running late. She needed to defend her championship title at the

World Jell-O Sculpture Contest. Twenty years ago, the judges had been completely amazed when

they saw her creation: a perfect replica of the Leaning Tower of Pisa, all made of lemon Jell-O.

Everyone wondered how she got the Jell-O to lean over like that without falling. She never

revealed her secret.

Still, she freely shared other secrets of Jell-O sculpture, so other contestants saw her as very

(3)_____, except when it came to the Leaning Tower. Every year for

20 years, she had constructed a new Leaning Tower, and every year for 20 years, she had

won.

"Vegetables
are a must on a
diet. I suggest carrot
cake, zucchini bread,
and pumpkin pie."

—Jim Davis

Nancy's cab stopped in front of the hotel, and she quickly paid the

cab fare. Walking briskly into the hotel lobby, a judge looked at her

sternly. "It is only one minute until contest time," he chided. "You

are almost late."

Name _____

JELL-O SCULPTURE CONTEST, CONTINUED

"So what? You can't start without *me*. I'm the champion. I'm the best! So get out of my way!"

The judge's mouth fell open. He was (4) _____ at Nancy's (5)_____ response. "Maybe we have let her get away with too much over the years," he thought. "We have chosen her for newspaper interviews, put her up in the best hotel rooms, and treated her to meals at four-star restaurants, just because she is the champion. Maybe we have (6)_____ her too much." He frowned as Nancy brushed past him and went to her stove and refrigerator. She began boiling water and opening 27 packets of Jell-O.

Meanwhile, another contestant, Betsy Billings, was wandering here and there around the contest area. She talked to other contestants, sat down to do a Sudoku puzzle, jumped up and opened a packet of Jell-O, sliced some bananas, and then went over to make a few calls on her cell phone. She giggled a lot. She wandered around a lot. She talked a lot. Nancy rolled her eyes and thought,

"What a (7)_____ . She's certainly not going to be any competition."

Calmly, Nancy created her twenty-first Leaning Tower of Pisa. Next to her, Clyde Culpepper was laboring intensely on his replica of a quarter horse. It was pathetic looking. Nancy pointed at it and (8)_____ . Nancy really wasn't a very nice person.

When the time limit was up, the judges began making their rounds. A crowd gathered around Betsy Billings' table. She had created a model of the Empire State Building, complete with King Kong on top and crowds of people on the streets below.

The judges didn't hesitate. Betsy won the grand championship.

"No one told me I could make people," cried Nancy. "I've been (9)_____ ." She burst into tears and was (10) _____ .

Betsy Billings just smiled. She wasn't such a (11)_____ after all.

BONUS. Write your own story using all 10 of the vocabulary words.

Name _____

CONFUSING THE CUSTOMERS

Below are some useful words to know. Using a dictionary for help, match the words on the left with the definitions on the right.

_____ 1. candor   a. difficult, strenuous
_____ 2. arduous   b. nonsense
_____ 3. negligible   c. to chatter or babble
_____ 4. malign   d. frankness, openness, sincerity
_____ 5. quibble   e. to silence, suppress, or crush
_____ 6. rapture   f. to speak unfavorably about, slander
_____ 7. flummoxed   g. full of great joy or delight
_____ 8. squelch   h. confused, perplexed
_____ 9. balderdash   i. small, trifling, unimportant
_____ 10. prattle   j. to argue over petty or irrelevant things

Read the story that follows and fill in the blanks with the appropriate words (or form of the words) from the list above. One word is used twice, the rest of them only once.

Confusing the Customers

Gilda worked part-time at Hot Dogs and Hamburgers "R" Us. She was a hard worker who always showed up on time, and she took her job very seriously. She got along with everyone— except for the customers. Gilda's boss, Mr. Shellingwellington, called her into his office.

"I have a serious problem with your performance," he said. Gilda looked (1) _____. She asked if she were getting fired.

"No," said Mr. Shellingwellington. "Not yet. But you are going to have to do something about the way you talk to customers. They are calling you snooty and rude."

"That's ridiculous!" cried Gilda. "They are (2)_____ my good name. You know that their comments are complete (3)_____."

"Complete *what*?" asked Mr. Shellingwellington.

"Never mind," said Gilda.

"See, Gilda, that's one of the problems that the customers have been complaining about. You use weird words that they don't understand."

Name _____

CONFUSING THE CUSTOMERS, CONTINUED

Gilda was mad. "So, am I supposed to (4)_____on and on about nothing instead?"

"Are you supposed to *what*?" asked Mr. Shellingwellington.

"Never mind," said Gilda.

Mr. Shellingwellington told Gilda she would have to (5)_____ her habit of using words their customers didn't understand. Then they wouldn't think she was snooty and rude. Gilda took a deep breath. She was fuming inside, but she told her boss that she appreciated his (6)_____ and said that she would try to improve.

She went to her station, and tried to smile, but she was worried. Then, a customer came up to the counter and ordered lunch. After she took the order, Gilda began to cheerily announce, as she always did, "We are most appreciative of your patronage." But then she stopped and changed her words. "Thank you," she said simply, and handed him his change.

He looked down at the two pennies. "I don't like to (7)_____ , but I should receive three cents change, not two. One penny may be a (an)(8)_____ amount to some, but I work hard for a living, working many hours at a (an) (9)_____ job that exhausts me. I do not relish the idea of thoughtlessly disposing of any monetary amount."

Gilda listened to him and smiled. "What kind of job was that?" she asked.

He repeated himself. "A (An) (10) _____ job."

Gilda smiled and sighed with (11)_____. Now *this* was a man she could fall for. "Would you mind lingering for a moment?" she asked. "I have to go retrieve someone. Do not vacate the premises, please!"

Gilda marched off to find Mr. Shellingwellington and tell him a thing or two. Then she was going to sit right down with this customer and introduce herself. She was sure they would have a lot to talk about.

 BONUS. Write your own story using all 10 of the vocabulary words.

What did one lab rat say to the other lab rat?

I sure have my scientist well-trained. All I have to do is push a buzzer, and he brings me a snack.

SUPPORTING WHAT YOU SAY

One of the mistakes people often make when writing or speaking on a subject important to them is *not* supporting what they say. They will say something like Harold did in a letter to the editor of the local newspaper:

> *I think fast food restaurants should be outlawed in this town. Our city council should get on the ball and get rid of them. I hate them.*

Harold definitely makes a point. However, he doesn't give any reasons why anyone should agree with him. Here's how he could make his point more effectively:

> *I think fast food restaurants should be outlawed in this town. First of all, most of the food in such restaurants is not healthy for our citizens to eat. Recent studies show that more and more children are overweight, and that is partly because of the fast food they eat, which is high in fat and calories. Getting rid of these restaurants would force citizens, including children, to have healthier eating habits.*
>
> *Second, fast food restaurants take away our town's individuality. With a string of fast food restaurants, our town looks like every other town of its size in America. Wouldn't it be much nicer to have a town with locally owned restaurants, with character? Wouldn't it be nice to be unique?*
>
> *Finally, getting rid of fast food restaurants would force people to stay at home more and eat. Young people would start learning how to cook again. Family members would talk to one another while preparing dinner. They would have family meals, thus strengthening family bonds and communication.*
>
> *It's clear that getting rid of fast food restaurants would have a positive effect on our community. I urge our city council to investigate this matter and to take action to improve the well-being of all who live here.*

This second version supports Harold's position with three clear points:

1. Fast food restaurants are not healthy.
2. Fast food restaurants take away a town's individuality.
3. The elimination of fast food restaurants would strengthen families.

(Whether you agree that these points are reasonable or smart is another question altogether!)

(continued)

"I will not eat oysters. I want my food dead—not sick, not wounded—dead."

—Woody Allen

SUPPORTING WHAT YOU SAY, CONTINUED

Practice coming up with ways to support a statement. Even though some of the statements below are rather ridiculous, see if you can come up with three points that support each. (Whenever you are trying to make a point, it's a good idea to have at least three things that support your position.)

Remember, you don't have to agree, personally, with the points you are making, below.

1. Subject: Fish make much better pets than cats.
    List three points that support this statement.

2. Subject: People should be required to go to school until age 30.
    List three points that support this statement.

3. Subject: Children should watch television for at least eight hours a day.
    List three points that support this statement.

4. Subject: Children should not be allowed to watch television at all.
    List three points that support this statement.

Name _____

REAL NICE, REAL GOOD

Good and *nice* are words that are used a lot. They usually indicate something positive, but they are so vague that they don't give much information. For example, imagine this conversation after a parent picks up her child:

"How was the birthday party?"
"Good."
"How was the food?
"Good."
"The new kid was there. What was he like?"
"Nice."
"How was the restaurant?"
"Nice."
"What else can you tell me about the party?"
"Jacob got some good presents. I had a nice time."

Sometimes, though, you can't even count on "good" and "nice" to indicate something positive. Imagine that your sister spills a glass of chocolate milk on your backpack.

"Real nice!" you say, sarcastically.

Or imagine that the computer crashes just before you save your report.

"Oh, good," you sigh, frustrated.

In general, more specific words convey a lot more information than the words *good* and *nice*. Look at how the birthday party conversation takes on a new life with more specific words:

"How was the birthday party?"
"Different than any party I've ever been to. The quarterback for the Broncos was there."
"How was the food?"
"The kind of stuff you'd get at a football game—hot dogs, nachos, pizza, Cokes."
"The new kid was there. What was he like?"
"He was friendly and really funny. He told a lot of jokes that made us laugh."
"How was the restaurant?"
"It had loud music, and there were huge posters of football stars everywhere."
"What else can you tell me about the party?"
"Jacob got some expensive presents, things I'd sure like to have. But the best part was talking to the Broncos quarterback and getting his autograph."

(continued)

Name _____

REAL NICE, REAL GOOD, CONTINUED

  Below are some descriptions of various scenes. Rewrite each, eliminating the words *good* and *nice* and using interesting details to create a vivid picture.

Scene #1

It was a good game. Everyone had a good time, and it was nice that our team won.

Scene #2

Claire took her little sister to a Disney movie. They had a nice time. They thought the movie was good. They had a nice time at the ice cream place afterwards. They had some good sundaes.

Scene #3

Brett went to a good dealership he knew about to find a nice used car. He found one at a good price. His wife thought it was nice. He thought it was good enough. He bought it.

Scene #4

Courtney looked around the dining room in the hotel. "This is nice," she thought.
"Good enough for me," said her sister.
"I'm sure we'll have a nice time here," said Courtney. "It will be a nice wedding reception."

"The difference between the almost right word and the right word is really a large matter— it's the difference between the lightning bug and the lightning."

—Mark Twain

Name _____

IN OTHER WORDS...

Paraphrasing means to put something in your own words. We do it all the time, even though we may not call it paraphrasing. For example, suppose your father says, "There is no way in the world that I'm going to let you go to a party and stay up until 1:00 a.m. on a school night, even if it is for your best friend's birthday and everyone else's parents are letting them go and you are the only one who won't be there and it will break her heart to have the party without you."

You are unlikely to repeat all that to your friend. You will probably *paraphrase* what your father said, perhaps like this: "My dad won't let me go to a party on a school night."

Paraphrasing isn't always *shorter* than the original material, but it is always *different*. It doesn't just substitute a word here and there. It generally uses a completely different sentence structure.

 Practice paraphrasing by putting the following information about sausage in your own words.

Except for vegetarians, most of us have eaten sausage. However, we probably didn't know much about what we were eating. Did you know, for example, that sausage was invented so that butchers had something to do with all the pieces and parts of an animal that didn't look all that appealing? For example, they would use scraps of meat, fat, blood, and organ meats such as brains, liver, tongue, and kidneys. They would stuff the mixture into actual animal intestines. It isn't exactly appetizing to think about. Today, however, most sausage is stuffed into casings made of cellulose, collagen, or even plastic.

The ingredients in sausage vary. Most European and Asian sausages are made up of 100% meat, fat, and spices. In the United States, there is a limit to how much of the sausage can be made up of fat. However, that limit is big—up to 50% of the weight of the sausage. (Rules vary, depending on the style of sausage.) The United States also prohibits the use of fillers like bread or other starch-based ingredients. In England, though, such fillers are common. They help the sausages keep their shape because they expand as the sausage heats up.

Countries all over the world make sausages, and there are hundreds of different kinds. Germany alone has over 1200 varieties. Some common varieties of sausage used in the U.S. are hot dogs, bratwurst, kielbasa, chorizo, and salami.

"Laws are like sausages. It is better not to see them being made."

—Otto von Bismarck

Name _____

IN FEWER WORDS...

Summarizing is a useful skill. When you summarize, you boil something down to its essential part. You tell only what is most important. For example, let's say you read this notice in the newspaper:

> The Lemon Paperclips will be performing at the Martinez Theater next Saturday at 8:00 p.m. This popular group consists of four women who play the guitar and sing. One reviewer described their music as "a cross between Janis Joplin, the Dixie Chicks, and Avril Lavigne, with just a touch of opera."
>
> The members of the group have been singing and playing together since they were 12 years old. Their records are very popular, especially with girls 12-18. They are known for songs about girls doing brave things, standing up for themselves, and being strong.
>
> The Lemon Paperclips are happy to be performing at Martinez Theater because of its great acoustics. Designed in 1999 by Gilbert Martinez, the theater is known for its wonderful sound, popular with audiences and performers alike.

Here's how someone might write a short summary of the information above:

> The popular group the Lemon Paperclips will be performing at the Martinez Theater next Saturday at 8:00 p.m. The four-woman group is especially popular with girls 12-18 and is known for its original songs about girls being strong.

Read the following newspaper story about the winner of the Cascades County Bake-Off Championship. Then write a summary of no more than 100 words. Make sure your summary includes what is most important about the story.

> Some people are surprised that Brutus Fowler bakes cakes—really, really good cakes. Fowler's cakes are so good that he won the Cascades County Bake-Off Championship on Saturday. But to look at him, you might think he was a wrestler, a rock star, or even a tattoo artist. He is six and a half feet tall, with thick, muscular arms covered with tattoos of snakes and skulls. You might be afraid if you ran into him in a dark alley, but you would be safe. "He's as gentle as a puppy dog," reports his girlfriend Allison Ginnelli.
>
> Fowler began baking cakes when he was only 12, to help his mother out in her bakery. He loved the work and started creating his own cake recipes. Soon her customers were asking for cakes by Brutus. One of the cakes he developed, Dark Chocolate Banana Dreamboat, is the one that took the grand championship at the Bake-Off. For his efforts, Fowler won $1,000 in cash and 25 pounds of sugar in the contest.

What do hungry computers eat?

Chips, one byte at a time.

Name _____

PARAPHRASE—AND SUM IT UP

You have learned that *paraphrasing* means putting something in your own words. (No, if you change "a" to "the," you aren't turning something into your own words. You need to *substantially* change whatever you are paraphrasing.)

You have also learned that *summarizing* means rewording and shortening something so that you are giving the essence or most important parts of it.

 Read the passage below. First, *paraphrase* it. Then *summarize* it in 100 words or less.

Some people are brave about foods. Chocolate covered ants? Sure, they will try them. A bit of raw octopus? Why not?

But it takes a truly adventurous person to eat a certain Japanese dish—fugu. Fugu is made from pufferfish, which contains the deadly poison tetrotoxin. If prepared incorrectly, fugu can kill a person, paralyzing the muscles while the victim remains conscious and slowly suffocates. There is no antidote for the poison, but some people do survive, especially those who hang on for the first 24 hours.

Because fugu is so dangerous, only specially licensed chefs are allowed to prepare it. They must work as apprentices for two to three years before being allowed to take the test for licensing. The test is so difficult that only 30% pass. The people who die from eating fugu are often people who try to cook it on their own, without any training.

In the past, some homeless people died from eating the poisonous parts of pufferfish discarded in restaurant trash cans. Therefore, the discarded parts must now be stored in locked barrels and later burned as hazardous waste. Even the knives used to prepare fugu must be special knives that are not allowed to touch any other foods.

One of the most famous fugu deaths occurred in 1975 when a famous Japanese actor visiting a restaurant insisted on eating four servings of the liver, the most poisonous part of the fish. The fugu chef didn't feel he could turn down such an important person. When the actor died, the chef lost his license.

"In Mexico we have a word for sushi: bait."

—José Simons

Name _____

PERSONIFYING FOOD

Mr. Stenner comes home late from work. His son says, "Let's go to a movie."

"Sorry," says Mr. Stenner. "My dinner is calling me."

We know, of course, that dinner can't call. What's it going to do? Shout, "Mr. Stenner! Mr. Stenner!" Wave at him? Make an "over here" gesture?

Of course not. Though he may not realize it, Mr. Stenner is using *personification*. In other words, he is giving human traits to an inanimate object. Here are two more examples:

The chocolate and the marshmallows kissed the graham crackers, becoming s'mores.

When Seth started jumping rope in the dining room, the dishes danced in the hutch.

Below are some verbs that express things that humans do. Choose verbs from this list and use them to write five sentences that *personify* foods. Be creative!

smile	frown	wink	watch
cackle	kiss	nod	hug
hurry	gobble	cough	laugh
sleep	whisper	sing	cry
knock	kick	tell	walk

Why did
the elephant
stand on the
marshmallow?

Because he
didn't want to fall into the
hot chocolate.

Name _____

HOW MANY WAYS...

 Answer the following:

1. How many ways can you find to say, "The food tasted great!" without saying, "The food tasted great"? List at least three.

2. How many ways can you find to say, "The movie was boring," without saying, "The movie was boring"? List at least three.

3. How many ways can you find to say, "It was an ugly dog," without saying, "It was an ugly dog"? List at least three.

What do you get when you put three ducks into a carton?

A box of quackers.

A SPOT OF PLOT

The setting: late at night outside a creepy old restaurant that has been closed for a long time
The characters: three young people

 You have the setting and the character basics. Now create a *plot*. What happens?

As you tell the story of what happens, make the last words of your sentences rhyme. The first and second sentences must rhyme. The second and third must rhyme. The fourth and fifth must rhyme, etc.

Here's an example of how one person started a story on a different subject:

> Frank hated to **babysit.** He really, really, really hated **it.** The worst was when he had to babysit his twin brother and sister, Katie and **Kyle.** The two were so wild that he had to be stern with them and could never **smile.** They found the Vaseline and smeared it all over their **hair**. It wouldn't come out, but Frank didn't **care**....

Your story should be at least 15 sentences long.

"My life has a superb cast but I can't figure out the plot."

—Ashleigh Brilliant

Name _____

GETTING HYPERBOLIC

"Why do I love my little Marshmallow Fluffster?" asked Liza, petting her little white kitten. "It's because she is the cutest little thing I ever saw! She's the most adorable cat that was ever born, and no one who sees her can resist her. She just oozes lovability, if that is a word. If it isn't a word, it should be because she is just SO lovable!"

Liza has a bad case of *hyperbole*. When people use hyperbole, they are exaggerating…a lot. Have some fun with hyperbole. First, describe your Aunt Eleanor's "chocolate decadence cake tower," using hyperbole.

Now that you are warmed up, choose one of the following and describe it in super awesome wonderful terms:

1. Your new kitchen

2. Your homemade pizza

3. Your new job as a celebrity chef

4. Your baby brother or sister's appetite

5. A class you are taking on gourmet cooking

6. Your talent at cooking

7. Someone else's talent at waiting tables

"Some folks never exaggerate— they just remember big."

—Audrey Snead

Name _____

SYNOPSIS TIME

You have just written a mystery called "Murder at the Café." You want to submit it to a publisher, hoping an editor there will like it and want to publish it. You are *sure* it will be a best seller.

You go to the guidbook *Writer's Market* and find that the publisher requires a *synopsis* of your book. You are baffled. You were under the impression that *synopsis* was some kind of drug used for treating stomach upset.

You are smart, though. You go to a dictionary and discover that a synopsis is not a drug at all. It is a brief summary of the plot of a novel, motion picture, play, etc. The synopsis tells what happens, without any frills or character development. Here, for example, is a synopsis of the fairy tale "Cinderella."

A king announces that a ball is to be held, and all unmarried young women in the kingdom are invited because the prince is looking for a wife. A young woman named Cinderella wants to go, but she can't because her wicked stepmother won't let her. She wants Cinderella to continue to clean the hearth and do other hard work around the home. Instead, she helps Cinderella's stepsisters get ready.

Cinderella makes a wish, though, and her fairy godmother makes her look like a princess, complete with a golden carriage to take her to the ball. She warns her, though, that she will turn back into her normal self at the stroke of midnight.

Cinderella goes to the ball, and the prince falls in love with her. When the clock starts to strike midnight, she runs away, leaving behind a glass slipper. The prince searches the kingdom to find the woman he loves, taking the glass slipper with him. When he gets to Cinderella's home, the shoe fits. The two get married and live happily ever after.

This synopsis tells the main plot of the fairy tale. Of course, it isn't very satisfying because all the good details are left out—the nastiness of the stepmother and the stepsisters, how forlorn and overworked Cinderella feels, the details of the clothes and carriage the fairy godmother creates with a flourish of her magic wand, etc. However, a synopsis is not *intended* to be a substitute for a story. It is just designed to tell the basics of the story, quickly.

 Write a one-page synopsis of *Murder at the Café.*

or

Write a one-page synopsis of a book you have read or a movie you have seen.

"In order to have a plot, you have to have a conflict. Something bad has to happen."

—Mike Judge

Name _____

EUPHEMISTICALLY SPEAKING

Marietta just made a hamburger for her boyfriend, Justin. He takes a bite and immediately realizes it is the worst burger he has ever eaten. He can barely swallow it because it is so dry. Still, when she asks him how it tastes, he doesn't want to hurt her feelings.

Luckily, Justin is good at using euphemisms—polite terms for something unpleasant. "Honey, I think this burger spent a little too much time on the grill. It's a bit moisture-challenged."

 The following items show Justin speaking euphemistically. Below each, write what he really means, but in blunt, straightforward terms.

1. Well, Grandma, little Fufu isn't going to be disturbing your sleep in the morning anymore. The vet found it was best to give her to an angel and let her fly up to that land of feather toys and all the tuna she can eat.

   What he really means: _____

   _____

2. Yes, indeed I certainly did read the manuscript for your new book. I am so impressed with your vocabulary! You certainly know a lot of big words. It is so interesting that you chose not to make plot an important part of the story—a brave choice. I certainly admire your courage! And I am impressed at your endurance. It may be the longest book I've ever read.

   What he really means: _____

   _____

Now *you* be the euphemistic one. You are a librarian, and you have to kick little Seneca Jones out of the library story time group. You have given her every chance in the world, but it is clear that she should not come again, ever, because she is out of control. She takes chocolate candy, warm, out of her pocket and gets it all over the rug and the books. She sings while you are trying to read. She pulls the hair of whatever little boy is unfortunate enough to be sitting next to her. She kicks people. She knocks over things. She talks too loud. She drives everyone crazy.
Write a letter to her mother and break the news that Seneca can no longer come to story time. Use euphemisms and the kindest language you can.

"I've had a wonderful evening—but this wasn't it."

—Groucho Marx

Name _____

PIZZA MONSTER

You are a writer for a movie studio. Your boss, in your opinion, has some of the dumbest ideas in the world. His latest? He wants to produce a movie about a pizza monster.

"What is a pizza monster?" you ask.

"That's for *you* to figure out!" he answers. "You create the monster. That's where we will start. Give me a one-page description of the monster. What does he look like? What are his monster-ish qualities? What is scary about him—or her? Oh, my, but you should have fun with this! I can't wait to read it."

 Write the one-page description. If you like, you can add a picture of your monster at the top. A few hints:

- Think of interesting verbs to describe what the monster does.

- Think of your senses. What does the monster look like? Sound like? Feel like? Smell like?

- What is really unusual about this monster? How does he differ from most other monsters you have seen in movies?

- Does the monster have any special powers?

"As far as I'm concerned, progress peaked with frozen pizza."

—From the movie *Die Hard 2*

Name _____

FOOD HOUSE

You have probably heard of *similes* and *metaphors*. A simile is an expression that compares one thing to another, using the words *like* or *as*. A metaphor is an expression that equates or compares two different things, without using the words *like* or *as*.

Here is an example of a simile:

Her hair was like a tornado, swirling around her head.

Here's an example of a metaphor:

His eyes were cameras, never missing a thing.

Imagine a home. Is it an old farm house? An apartment? A modern mansion? A cell block? A cozy cottage? A tent? Describe the home, using metaphors and similes that compare the house to food. Use at least seven similes and at least one metaphor. Here's an example of one way to start:

Antonio's house had a slick steel roof, as slick as a banana peeling on an icy sidewalk. The front door was as purple as a grape…

"Metaphors have a way of holding the most truth in the least space."

—Orson Scott Card

APLES AND ORENGES
s p e l l i n g

It's not easy to interest students in spelling. "Aples and Orenges" is an activity that will help them pay close attention. Students work in groups of two or three to try to create a spelling test that will receive the *worst* score from other students. By trying to create a hard test, with an answer key, they are forced to concentrate, hard, on spelling.

First ask each group to write a description or a short story called "What Happened at the Grocery Store." As students write, have them include spelling mistakes—a total of 50 of them. (Or, depending on your students, you might want them to try for 100 errors.) Suggest that they try not to be too obvious. For example, they might not want to spell *can of corn* as *cn of crn*. Suggest that they also include some words that people often have trouble with, like *there, they're* and *their* and *to, two,* and *too.* They will also want to be sure their story is still readable. A sentence with *too* many errors may be impossible to correct, as no one can tell what was even intended. (Example: *Cidz plyng wth knzuf fud 'n maikng twers inthe iles where mackng custmrz tns.*)

When students have finished their stories full of errors, they then create answer keys. (The answer keys must be on a separate page.)

Now the fun begins. Each group gives its error-filled story to another group. The other group does its best to correct all the errors. When it is finished correcting, it gives the corrected paper back to the original group to score.

Here's where things can get interesting. The original group must give the scored paper *back* to the correctors, *with* the answer key, and give them a chance to check the scoring group's work. If the group members find a mistake on the answer key, they get two points back. Thus, both the originators of the piece and the correctors of the piece have a chance to gain and lose points.

No, the game won't turn your students into perfect spellers. However, it will help them learn to be more aware of spelling. And they may even learn a thing or two as they complete this activity.

PICK ONE
r e l e v a n t   d e t a i l s

This is an exercise in choosing *relevant* details. First, ask students to pick one of the following topics.

salt, pizza, cereal, a particular fast food restaurant, Thanksgiving dinner

Then give students five minutes to write down absolutely everything they can think of about their topic—*everything*. They should write as fast as possible.

After five minutes, ask students to stop and read over what they have written. Then explain that you are going to give them three more minutes. They should stretch their brains and see if there is anything else they can say on their topic. Remind them that they should write down anything they can think of even remotely related to their topic.

Then have students look over what they have written again. It is likely that a lot of what they have written is rather dull. Ask, "What is *most* interesting to you? What surprises you? What is funny?"

Finally, ask students to pull out something from what they have written and use it as the basis of one *focused* paragraph. Remind them that they may use anything they have already written but should leave out details that don't relate to the subject of their paragraph. They are likely to need to add other details to develop the topic of the paragraph.

CLICHÉ

We all use *clichés*. *Clichés* are standard words and phrases that we use without even thinking. For example, when someone wants to say a boy is acting just like his dad would in similar circumstances, the person might say, "He's a **chip off the old block**." *Chip off the old block* is a cliché. Here are some more examples of clichés:

*She loses her temper **at the drop of a hat.***

*He's such a genereous guy. He'd **give you the shirt off his back.***

The problem with clichés is that they are so worn-out from overuse that they don't always convey a lot of meaning. Replacing them with new, fresh phrases can make writing more interesting. The sentences above might be rewritten like this, for example:

She loses his temper over just about anything,
even a drop of water spilled on the counter.

He's such a generous guy that if he had only a can of green beans left to eat
in all the world and you needed it, he would hand it right over.

 Below is a story filled with clichés. Underline all 14 of them.

"I just made the best cookies I've ever tasted!" said Marcella.

"Well, you're sure tooting your own horn," said her sister Carmen. "I'll bet I've made plenty of cookies that are just as good."

"I doubt it. These were special. I threw in just about everything but the kitchen sink, so they cost an arm and a leg. They may be expensive, but they are definitely worth it."

"Let's have a contest. Let's both bake another batch, and if my cookies aren't as good as yours, I'll eat my hat." Carmen was madder than a wet hen. She hated how her sister was always bragging. "I could beat her with one hand tied behind my back," she thought.

"Could I get a word in edgewise?" interrupted their mother. "I hate to rain on your parade, but we are not having a cookie baking contest in this kitchen. If you two have time on your hands, I've got three closets that need to be cleaned, and many hands make light work, you know."

The girls looked at each other. "Hold your horses, Mom," said Carmen. "We were just kidding around. Let's not make a mountain out of a molehill."

"Let's put that contest on the back burner for now," said Marcella.

"Well, no one can ever say you two are hard workers," said Mom, "although you may be fast thinkers."

 Now rewrite the story, eliminating the clichés and replacing them with more descriptive wording.

> "A balanced diet is a cookie in each hand."
>
> —Author Unknown

Name _____

WATCHING A CHARACTER

Good writers usually tell about characters through their *actions*. Instead of writing that the hero of the story "is an athletic guy who is very strong," the writer is more likely to write something like this:

*Bruno tossed bales of hay on to the haystack, hoping to finish in time
to go for a three-mile run before dinner.*

The above sentence tells us, through his actions, something about Bruno. A weak little guy would probably not be tossing around bales of hay. Knowing that he wants to run tells us that he is probably physically fit, especially if he's running for three miles.

Imagine a character of your own. Is it a child? A teenager? An adult? What kind of personality does he or she have? Is the person generous, selfish, boring, happy, pessimistic, optimistic, beautiful, handsome, old, young, conceited, shy, talkative, rude, kind, or what?

Think about the character and then create a situation involving your character eating or serving food. By writing about what your character *does,* tell us at least two important things about the person. Don't *tell* us what the character is like. *Show* us.

"Action speaks
louder than words
but not nearly
as often."

—Mark Twain

STRAIN YOUR BRAIN #1

 Complete the following:

1. Write a sentence in which every single word starts with either "a" or "m." The sentence must be at least 8 words long and involve food.

2. Put this sentence in a short paragraph where it makes sense: *Finnegan felt foolish looking at the fettuccini.*

3. Write one paragraph that uses all these words: *banana, purred, spaghetti, lawn mower, blender, lemon.*

4. Write three sentences that use the word *sipped.* Create a completely different picture with each sentence.

5. Your company is selling *Plinkmottle.* In one paragraph, describe Plinkmottle so that (a) we know what it is and (b) it sounds desirable. Don't *tell* us what it is, though.

Lisa: "Do we have any food that wasn't brutally slaughtered?" Homer: "Well, I think the veal died of loneliness."

—*The Simpsons* by Matt Groening

STRAIN YOUR BRAIN #2

 Complete the following:

1. Write a paragraph about a food you feel strongly about, whether you love it or hate it. Start with a three-word sentence. Follow it with a four-word sentence, then a five-word sentence, then a six-word sentence, then a seven-word sentence, and an eight-word sentence. Each sentence must begin differently. (You can't write, "I hate peas," followed by, "I hate peas intensely." You *could* write, "I hate peas," followed by, "They are so disgusting."

2. Write a sentence in which the only vowel used is "e." The sentence must be at least 7 words long.

3. Write a paragraph about milk, using only one-syllable words. The paragraph must be at least five sentences long.

4. Name 8 things you might find in a refrigerator.

5. For each item in #8, write a sentence beginning with that item. The verb in each sentence *cannot* be "is" or "are."

"I don't drown
my sorrows;
I suffocate them
with chocolate
chip cookies."

—Author Unknown

Name _____

BARE BONES

Writing is much more effective when it includes interesting details and specific words. For example, compare these two sentences that give the same basic information, but in different ways:

The teacher yelled at the boy.

When Calvin interrupted the lesson by coming in late, again,
Mr. Featherstone erupted, thundering so loudly at Calvin about his irresponsible attitude
that he disrupted the band rehearsing next door.

Obviously, the second sentence is much more interesting and helps us picture what happened.

Below are some bare-bones sentences—sentences that contain only very basic information. Rewrite each sentence, keeping the same essential facts but adding details to make it much more interesting.

1. They watched the person throw the food.

2. He cooked his first meal.

3. She served the food.

4. He tasted the food.

5. They grew food.

Who won
the skeleton
beauty contest?

No body.

Name _____

COMPOUNDS

Compound is an interesting word. It can mean so many different things. As a noun, it can refer to a fenced-in group of buildings, like the *presidential compound.* If you break an arm or a leg and the bone is sticking through the skin, you have a *compound* fracture. A *compound* word is a word made of two words, like *rowboat.* If whatever you do to help a situation ends up *compounding* the problem, you made it worse.

Sentences can involve *compounds,* too. A sentence with a compound subject has two subjects. (An example: **Thomas** and **Terry** fought Queen Kong.) A sentence with a compound predicate has two predicates. (Example: Thomas **fought** Queen Kong and **captured** her.) Sometimes a sentence has both a compound subject and a compound predicate. (**Thomas** and **Terry** *fought* Queen Kong and *captured* her.)

A compound sentence is really *two* sentences that are connected by one of these words: *and, but, or, for, nor, so, yet.* (Examples: Thomas fought Queen Kong, but Terry captured her.)

And, finally, a compound sentence might also have a compound subject and/or a compound predicate. (**Thomas** and **Terry** *fought* Queen Kong and *captured* her, but **Queen Kong** and her **husband** *escaped* and *terrified* the entire city.)

 Add the compounds indicated for each sentence below.

1. Henry ate the chocolate covered grasshoppers. (Add a compound subject.)

_____

2. Henry ate the chocolate covered grasshoppers. (Add a compound predicate.)

_____

3. Henry ate the chocolate covered grasshoppers. (Make the sentence a compound sentence.)

_____

Identify the compounds in the sentences on the next page.

- no compounds
- compound subject
- compound predicate
- both a compound subject and a compound predicate
- compound sentence

Name _____

COMPOUNDS, CONTINUED

- compound sentence with a compound subject or a compound predicate.
- compound sentence with both a compound subject and a compound predicate

1. Pete absolutely loves his rabbit, Nuzzles, and he also loves his tarantula, Elmer.

2. Melissa absolutely loves Nuzzles, but she despises Elmer.

3. Pete and Melissa both love Mr. Ellington, their cat.

4. Mr. Ellington hates Nuzzles, and he hates Elmer, too.

5. Mr. Ellington hates pretty much everybody.

6. Pete and Melissa worried and fussed about Mr. Ellington, but Nuzzles and Elmer ignored him and slept a lot.

7. Mr. Ellington ignored them back.

8. He ignored Pete, and he ignored Melissa, too.

9. He was the leader of the pack, and he liked it that way.

10. Pete and Melissa bought a kitten for Mr. Ellington.

11. They named the kitten Cutikens and introduced her to Mr. Ellington.

12. Mr. Ellington hissed and scratched, and Cutikens yowled at Mr. Ellington and jumped on his back.

13. Mr. Ellington was not happy.

14. Cutikens did not care, and she chased him into the closet and yowled some more.

15. Now Cutikens is the leader of the pack.

What do you call
artificial spaghetti?

Mockaroni.

Name _____

IN THE NEWS

Writing newspaper-style is different from most other kinds of writing. First of all, it follows a definite pattern: the first sentence or two nearly always answers these questions: Who? What? Where? When? Why? and sometimes How?

Newspaper writers include the most important information first and then move to the least important details. This method of news writing is called the "inverted pyramid."

Because of limited space, news articles generally don't include a lot of extra information. They also don't give the writer's opinion. They use simple language. They keep it short.

News writing differs from most other types of writing because the mission is to deliver the facts as quickly as possible. Let's look at the difference.

Suppose there is a fire in a restaurant. Here's how Samantha might describe it in an e-mail to her aunt:

Dear Aunt Sylvia,

We all went to a new restaurant in town this weekend. It was Dad's birthday, you know, so we wanted to go somewhere special. Dad wanted to give this new place a try. I was like, no way! I mean, the name is totally cheesy: Stanley's Super Duper Buffet. But Dad insisted. You know how he gets.

Anyway, Super Duper Buffet is in the building where the old movie theater was. Remember it? I loved going there with you to see the latest movies—what was the last flick we saw there? I can't remember. If you can think of it, let me know. Well, the new restaurant was really good, even though the name is pretty lame. They had everything you could think of, from roast pig to candied apples. I know how much you love candied apples. The next time you visit, we'll have to go there. You will love it!

The only thing is, there was a little accident in the kitchen while we were there. Luckily, it happened after we were finished stuffing our faces. The manager came running out of the kitchen, yelling for everyone to evacuate immediately. The head chef had accidentally started a large fire in one of the kitchen's garbage cans. I guess they got it under control eventually. Weird. Anyway, I hope you will visit soon!

Love,
Sally

IN THE NEWS, CONTINUED

However, if Sally were writing a newspaper article, her account might sound like this:

On Saturday evening at 7:35, customers at Stanley's Super Duper Buffet were evacuated because of a fire. The fire was started accidentally by head chef Pilton Wheezeguard. The fire department responded promptly and got the blaze under control. No one was injured.

Super Duper Buffet opened just last month in the space where the Luxe Theatre used to be, at the corner of 5th and Market.

 Now, read the news story below. Then rewrite the article, following the rules outlined above.

Escaped Boa Constrictor Causes Chaos

Sternbladt Junior High is located on the corner of Whitcomb and Plumberry. My brother went to school there. Anyway, the school was a chaotic scene on Friday. Friday is the favorite day of many students. I've always liked Fridays, myself. The students must have been enjoying their Friday school day, too. Around lunch time, the students filed into the cafeteria. Everything was quiet and normal until the boa constrictor escaped from the science lab and slithered into the lunch room. Apparently, someone had left the door of its cage open. All of the students were enjoying their spaghetti and meatballs when the snake was spotted. Soon, pasta was flying. Meatballs were rolling. Sauce was splattering. The students were screaming and throwing their lunch trays. One minute, someone saw the boa constrictor over by the milk machine. The next minute, someone saw it under their table. Panic had set in, and chaos ruled. The snake had gone into the kitchen, but no one knew it at the time. The students were still in a state of shock. Some of them were standing on the lunch tables. Others had fled the scene. Then, the lunch ladies came running out of the kitchen. Finally, the science teacher, along with the help of the gym teacher, caught the boa constrictor and put an end to the chaos in the lunch room. No one finished their lunch, though.

"Television has raised writing to a new low."

—Samuel Goldwyn

MS. PERSNICKETY

an english teacher's pet peeves

If your students are like most, they zone out when it comes to talking about the conventions of language. The difference between *their, they're,* and *there?* They don't want to hear it. It's bor-r-r-r-i-n-g.

For a change, challenge them to *break* the rules. In the student section of "Ms. Persnickety Needs Help" are listed 25 of Ms. Persnickety's (and most English teachers') pet peeves. Your students have undoubtedly heard these before, so don't bother going over them. Even if there are items they haven't heard before, that's okay.

Simply read the instructions with the students and emphasize that for Ms. Persnickety's test, they must "commit" every single one of Ms. Persnickety's pet peeves. Explain that they can help each other and that you will be available for help or clarification if they need it. (How refreshing it will be to have them come to *you* for help in really understanding an item!)

This is an excellent activity for group work. Allow students to work in small groups of two or three. And don't drive yourself crazy grading these assignments. After students turn them in, pass them back out for other groups to "grade." Each group will check to see that each item on another group's paper is used incorrectly—another reinforcement of the rules. (Students have to know what a rule *is* in order to break it.) Be available to settle any disagreements.

And then follow up with Ms. Persnickety in a Devious Mood. In this activity, some of the items from the pet peeve list are used correctly, and some are used incorrectly. This time students work to make the entire story *correct*.

Name _____

MS. PERSNICKETY NEEDS HELP

Ms. Persnickety is just like a lot of English teachers. She has a number of pet peeves about writing. Here are just 25 of them:

1. Mixing up *it's* and *its*.
2. Confusing *your* and *you're*.
3. Using *to* and *too* incorrectly.
4. Writing *coulda, shoulda, woulda* instead of *could have, should have, would have*.
5. Spelling *a lot* as one word.
6. Mixing up *they're, there,* and *their*.
7. Using casual spellings like *'cuz* in formal writing.
8. Using symbols like "&" instead of *and* or *$$$* instead of *money* in formal writing.
9. Writing *I seen* instead of *I saw*.
10. Writing *kinda, sorta,* and *hafta* instead of *kind of, sort of,* and *have to*.
11. Starting sentence after sentence with *well* or *so* or *then*.
12. Writing *me and my friends* instead of *my friends and I*.
13. Writing *go* instead of *said* (He goes, "yes," and I go, "no.").
14. Using *and stuff* instead of specific examples.
15. Writing *use to* instead of *used to* and *suppose to* instead of *supposed to*.
16. Writing *supposebly* instead of *supposedly*.
17. Misspelling *etc.* as *ect*.
18. Writing *expecially* and *excape* instead of *especially* and *escape*.
19. Mixing up *lose* and *loose*.
20. Mixing up *whose* and *who's*.
21. Separating two sentences with only a comma, thus creating a run-on sentence.
22. Mixing up *lead* and *led*.
23. Writing *alright* instead of *all right*.
24. Writing *gotta, gonna, wanna* instead of *got to, going to,* and *want to*.
25. Mixing up *quiet* and *quite*.

Ms. Persnickety needs to write a test, but she just can't bring herself to write a story full of errors for her students to correct. Do it for her. Write a story involving a school cafeteria, and see if you can include every single one of Ms. Persnickety's pet peeves. Make sure everything in all 25 items above is used *incorrectly*. Don't allow even one of the items to be used correctly. Your score will be reduced if you use even one term from her pet peeve list correctly!

So, just this once, break all the rules!

"I never made a mistake in grammar but one in my life and as soon as I done it I seen it."

—Carl Sandburg

MS. PERSNICKETY GETS TESTY

Ms. Persnickety has already talked, a *lot,* about 25 of her pet peeves about writing. Yet a student just turned in a paper called "Dead Mouse" that shows he has not been paying attention at all. Ms. Persnickety has decided that his paper will make a perfect test for her students.

See how *you* do on Ms. Persnickety's test. In the story below, some things are used correctly, and some are used incorrectly. Your job is to go through the story, circle all the errors, and correct them. There are 37 errors in the story. Can you find them all?

"There's a dead mouse in my soup!" cried Mr. Evanovitch. He thought he was going to throw up. "In fact, there are *two* dead mice in my soup," he added. " Their both kinda gray and sort of shriveled up."

"I don't think it's expecially disgusting," said the waiter, whose name was Charles, as he peered into the soup. He goes, "Its certainly nothing to loose you're lunch over. We get alot of mice in the soup here."

Well, Mr. Evanovitch certainly wasn't too happy to hear that, he just couldn't believe it. Well, he just didn't know what 2 say for a moment, he was so shocked. "Me and my friends have wanted too come here for a long time, supposebly this is one of the best restaurants in town. I've always heard it was quiet nice, but its certainly *not.*"

"The soup may not be so good, but we've got the best desserts in town," said Charles. "No mice in the desserts at all. If you'd like 4 me to get you one, I'll be happy too."

Mr. Evanovitch was horrified. "I can't believe I seen mice in my soup, and you aren't even upset. I wanna see the manager!"

"Alright," said Charles. "I don't think she'll be to happy, though. She's gotta lot of work to do." So he went off to find Mrs. Hampshire, she was in her office in the back. So he told her what happened and stuff.

"I know I'm suppose to run right out there," sighed Mrs. Hampshire, "but what I'd really like to do is escape. I could really use a hot bath, a massage, a warm cup of cocoa, etc. Its no fun being the manager sometimes. I shoulda been a nurse. I use to like science and stuff in school. I would have been happier, I think, as a nurse. " She looked at Charles and sighed again. "I know I have to go out there." She got up, & Charles lead her out front to Mr. Evanovitch.

Mr. Evanovitch was so upset he couldn't even speak. He just made funny noises in his throat.

"How about a nice piece of pie," said Mrs. Hampshire. She gave him her most winning smile.

"I'm not a very good writer, but I'm an excellent rewriter."

—James Michener

Name _____

DDN SHOW

The new president of the Delicious Dining Network (DDN) wants to take the network in a new direction. "All the dishes on every program look *great*," she said. "In fact, they look so great that they don't seem so great. After all, if everyone you look at is drop dead gorgeous, the least gorgeous of them is not going to look so good. The same thing is happening with our food shows. Some great looking dishes don't look so great when they are compared with dishes that look even better. Make sense?"

Well, you're not sure. But you do know she has hired you to come up with some dishes that don't look great on television. You decided on one dish already: Monochromatic Oatmeal. You describe it as "oatmeal with chunks of banana, served in a gray bowl that is sitting on a beige tablecloth."

She loves it. "This is great," she said. "The host of Breakfast Delights can now say to viewers, 'You choose. Do you want to serve your family Monochromatic Oatmeal or my Blueberry Delight scones with red rasberry jelly and lemon yogurt?"

 Create five more dishes that look bad. Name each dish and describe it carefully. Remember, you want to please the president!

ANSWER KEY

Note: Many *Language Is Served* activities do not have a single right or wrong answer. On the activities where answers will vary, we have included sample answers. These samples are provided because many teachers find them helpful. However, they are not intended to be models—just examples of one way to correctly complete each activity's requirements.

HEALTHY SCRAMBLING, PAGE 7

1. strawberries
2. yogurt
3. lettuce
4. chicken
5. fish
6. carrots
7. milk
8. bread
9. grapefruit
10. almonds
11. cereal
12. pasta (or tapas)
13. eggs
14. onions
15. mushrooms
16. jalapenos
17. garbanzo beans
18. peaches
19. olives
20. artichokes
21. lean pork
22. red pepper
23. cucumber
24. ginger
25. asparagus
26. bananas
27. tofu
28. broccoli
29. spinach
30. yams
31. oranges
32. apples
33. garlic
34. olive oil
35. tomatoes
36. turkey
37. blueberries
38. beets
39. brussels sprouts
40. prunes
41. raisins
42. oatmeal
43. potatoes
44. cauliflower
45. pumpkins
46. brown rice
47. eggplant
48. corn
49. turnip greens
50. barley

CHOCOLATE MASHED POTATOES, PAGE 8

Answers will vary. Sample answer:

White Vegetables

My little brother Aaron hated vegetables when he was a kid. He preferred meals of the meat and bread variety. The only vegetables he would eat were potatoes—in mashed or fried form. Mom was always trying to get him to eat more vegetables. She would make things that combined meat and vegetables so it would be harder for him to avoid eating them.

Once, Mom made chicken and vegetable stir-fry for dinner. Aaron winced when she set down the bowl in the center of the table. Mom's reaction to this was to tell him he had to at least try it.

"Okaaay," he said, frowning.

We all began eating, including Aaron, who picked reluctantly at a tiny little pile of stir-fry on his plate. We were all silent as we enjoyed the delicious meal.

Then Aaron started dishing up seconds. Mom, surprised, asked, "Do you like it?"

He tilted his head a little and raised his eyebrows. "I *really* like the white vegetables."

"The white vegetables?" Mom asked.

"Yeah. These," he said, pointing to a piece of stir-fry on his plate.

Mom burst out laughing and dropped her fork, which clattered loudly on her plate.

"What!?" Aaron said.

"That's the chicken!" Mom said, and we all laughed.

The funny thing is, Aaron turned into a vegetarian shortly after he went off to college. But after he graduated, he went back to his meat-eating ways. I guess we develop our tastes at a young age.

ANSWER KEY

SYLLABLE CHALLENGE, PAGE 9

Answers will vary. Sample answers:

One-syllable words	Two-syllable words	Three-syllable words	Four-Syllable Words
1. soup	1. waffle	1. banana	1. huckleberry
2. milk	2. spinach	2. potato	2. cauliflower
3. eggs	3. lettuce	3. strawberry	3. pomegranate
4. beets	4. pepper	4. tortilla	4. avocado
5. leeks	5. onion	5. broccoli	5. watermelon
6. cheese	6. scallion	6. blueberry	6. rutabaga
7. beans	7. cabbage	7. casserole	7. macaroni
8. bread	8. apple	8. tomato	8. fettucini
9. cake	9. pancake	9. cucumber	9. ravioli
10. pop	10. yogurt	10. cantaloupe	10. tortellini
11. peas	11. bacon	11. pineapple	SUBTOTAL: 40
12. peach	12. sausage	12. artichoke	
13. squash	13. syrup	13. zucchini	
14. yam	14. sandwich	14. horseradish	
15. fish	15. cracker	15. honeydew	
16. toast	16. pretzel	16. mayonaise	
17. grape	17. candy	17. lasagna	
18. lime	18. cookie	18. hamburger	
19. cream	19. soda	19. cereal	
20. beef	20. orange	20. marshmallow	
21. pork	21. radish	21. cranberry	
22. crab	22. mango	22. halibut	
23. stew	23. kiwi	23. burrito	
24. trout	24. turnip	SUBTOTAL: 69	
25. pie	25. carrot		
26. roll	26. mushroom		
27. fudge	27. honey		
SUBTOTAL: 27	28. lobster		
	29. oatmeal		
	30. pasta		
	31. grapefruit		
	32. eggplant		
	33. muffin		
	34. salad		
	35. bagel		
	36. popcorn		
	SUBTOTAL: 72		

ANSWER KEY

ANSWER KEY

HELP HUNGRY HENRY'S, PAGE 10

Answers will vary. Sample answers:

Fabulous Fried Chicken: We dip our tender, free-range chicken in rich, flavorful batter and then deep-fry it in healthy canola oil until it's perfectly crispy.

No-More-Hunger Hamburger: Try our natural, handmade ground beef patty, cooked to your liking with a generous smothering of extra sharp cheddar cheese and then topped with fresh lettuce, homemade pickles, and slices of organic onion and garden-fresh tomato.

Super Dog: We grill a delicious 100% beef hot dog and then serve it on a fresh bun with sweet chopped onion and tangy relish.

More-Than-Just Mashed Potatoes: We use locally grown organic red potatoes, the freshest milk money can buy, and hand-churned butter to make our mashers creamy and sweet.

Ranch Style Home Fries: Only the best russet potatoes from the farm down the road are used to make our hand-cut, ranch style fries, which we cook until perfectly crisp on the outside and tender in the middle.

Grandma's Green Beans: We add smoked bacon and onions to our garden-fresh green beans and then slowly bake them until they're tender and savory.

Captivating Coleslaw: We make our coleslaw fresh every morning, using only the finest organic cabbages and carrots to make a creamy, crunchy coleslaw with just a hint of horseradish for spice.

DON'T KNOCK IT UNTIL YOU TRY IT, PAGE 11

Answers will vary. Sample answers:

1. hakarl – fermented or cured shark meat.
   Although wimpy foreigners don't like hakarl, we Icelanders love the strong, pungent taste of cured shark meat. It is similar in appearance and texture to the meat jerky found in other countries, but is much more robust and flavorful. It's best served with an ice cold drink.
2. scrapple – a seasoned mixture of cornmeal, pork scraps and trimmings, set in a mold and served sliced and fried..
   This dish is the perfect side for scrambled eggs. The cornmeal and ham mixture is sliced and fried until brown and crispy and is perfect with syrup or apple butter. Yum!
3. escargot – cooked snails.
   Escargot cooked in butter and salt is tender and delectably mild with a flavor like mushrooms and scallops.
4. chitterlings – fried hog intestines.
   Chitterlings taste great with ketchup. They are as crispy as fried onions and slightly chewy, like clam meat. Delicious!
5. poi – taro root, cooked, pounded and kneaded to a paste, often allowed to ferment.
   Poi is as smooth as ice cream and has the sweetest flavor, a flavor that reminds me of tapioca pudding.
6. haggis – heart, liver and lung of sheep or calf, minced with suet, onions, oatmeal and seasonings and boiled in the stomach of the sheep or calf.

Scottish haggis has a wonderful nutty texture and a savory taste that is *so* much better than plain old sausage.

7. lutefisk – dried codfish soaked in water and lye.

    For an unusual dining experience, you can't go wrong with lutefisk. With its uniquely pungent flavor and soft jelly-like texture, it tastes great with melted butter.

8. kimchi – pickled vegetables seasoned with garlic, red pepper and ginger.

    The pickled vegetables in kimchi are hot and spicy and bursting with the flavors of garlic, red pepper and ginger. Your taste buds will sit up and take notice!

HUNGER, PAGE 12

Answers will vary. Sample answer:

Almost half of the ten hunger organizations listed are very well known, well established, four-star rated groups with enormous budgets. They provide food, medical care, education and other services to the poorest people in countries around the world, including the U.S.

The other groups are smaller and vary widely. Two of them, I think, would really benefit from a $10,000 donation, and it would be really clear where the money would be used and who would be helped.

Project Peanut Butter is based in Malawi, possibly the poorest country in South Africa, and Meds and Food for Kids is based in Haiti, the poorest country in the western hemisphere. Both were founded by pediatricians on the faculty of Washington University School of Medicine. These are organizations that really focus on saving children under five years old, especially the most vulnerable ones from 6-18 months of age. In these poor countries, babies survive on their mother's milk, and older children get what little food there is. That leaves small toddlers left with little or nothing to eat, and that puts them at highest risk for starvation.

Project Peanut Butter and Meds and Food for Kids provide something called Ready to Use Therapeutic Food, known as RUTF, for severely malnourished young children. RUTF is a peanut based formula fortified with milk powder, oil, sugar and a vitamin/mineral compound. Enough RUTF is given to mothers to take home and feed their young children daily for a six week course. The cost for this treatment is about $83.00 per child, or less than $2.00 per day. These two organizations are administered by all volunteer staffs and employ citizens of Malawi and Haiti to produce the RUTF. The recovery rate for young children who receive treatment with RUTF is 80-90%.

While it's great to contribute to any of the organizations, with many of them you never know exactly where or how your donation is going to be used. With Project Peanut Butter and Meds and Food for Kids, you know that your money is going directly to feed kids that really need help.

BEWARE OF "BECAUSE," PAGE 13

Answers will vary. Sample answers:

1. She hated to go out to eat with the Barton family because she hated seeing Gil chew with his mouth open.

    Because she hated seeing Gil chew with his mouth open, she ate in her bedroom, alone.

2. Dave worked 18-hour days because he wanted to grow perfect watermelons.

    Because he wanted to grow perfect watermelons, Dave drove his workers hard.

3. Gracie studied night and day because she wanted to go to medical school someday.
   Because she wanted to go to medical school someday, Gracie was never satisfied with a "B+."
4. He almost lost his lunch because of the bug floating in his chocolate shake.
   Because of the bug floating in his chocolate shake, Sam decided he didn't want to eat at Rachel's house anymore.

SIZZLING SYNONYMS, PAGE 14

Answers will vary. Sample answers:

1. good/tasty	8. crisp/brittle	15. bland/dull	22. soggy/damp
2. spicy/zesty	9. dark/black	16. weak/watery	23. soft/spongy
3. crunchy/flaky	10. strong/tough	17. dry/crumbly	24. light/mild
4. raw/uncooked	11. warm/toasty	18. spoiled/bad	25. tasteless/plain
5. sweet/sugary	12. chewy/rubbery	19. sour/tangy	
6. frozen/icy	13. lumpy/chunky	20. runny/thin	
7. thick/dense	14. cold/frosty	21. creamy/smooth	

1. That extra long Coney dog with extra cheese and onions was tasty.
2. The zesty sauce made my lips burn.
3. I love the flaky crust of a freshly baked croissant.
4. Every day for lunch, Alice eats uncooked broccoli dipped in hot cheese sauce.
5. Lee stared at the sugary donuts, wishing he hadn't spent all of his money.
6. There's nothing like an icy glass of lemonade on a hot day.
7. The cheesecake was so dense it stuck to my fork like glue.
8. My brother loves peanut brittle candy.
9. My dad takes his coffee black, even when the coffee tastes terrible.
10. Don't overcook the steak or it will become too tough.
11. The fresh bread was toasty.
12. The meat was so rubbery that I couldn't bite into it.
13. Joseph will only eat chunky salsa.
14. He handed me a giant frosty mug of root beer.
15. I'm tired of the same old dull meat and potatoes dinner!
16. The soup is much too watery.
17. The cake was so crumbly I had to eat it with a spoon.
18. The cottage cheese had gone bad.
19. The fresh necatarines were tangy and sweet.
20. He likes his oatmeal thin.
21. Stir the lemon meringue until it's whipped into a smooth consistency.
22. The loaf of bread got damp in the bottom of the picnic basket.
23. The spongy texture of tofu is hard for some to get used to.
24. Anything hotter than a mild pepper is hard on my stomach.
25. Who likes plain yogurt?

ANSWER KEY

ANSWER KEY

D-D-DOUG'S D-D-DELIGHT, PAGE 15

Answers will vary. Sample answers:

1. Delectable Dumplings
2. Duckling with Dressing
3. Dish of Dairy Delights
4. Denver Omelet
5. Divine Deli Plate
6. Doug's Dinner Rolls
7. Dover Sole with Dill
8. Deluxe Dried Mushrooms
9. Delicious Dijon Mustard Tenderloin
10. Dessert of Dark Dollops of Delicious Chocolate Drizzled on Dates

Where can you go to delight *your* darling this December? If you desire to dine with a divine selection of delicious food and drink, don't delay in driving out to Doug Dougenhoffer's Denver Dining Delight, located at Diamond Divide Road. You'll discover dozens of delectable dishes to delight your tastebuds, and you'll definitely devour the decadent desserts. You'll be doubly delighted at the disco style decor, and you'll enjoy dancing after your dining experience. Doug Dougenhoffer's Denver Dining Delight is definitely the direct path to dining decadence. Call now for reservations!

FIXER UPPER, PAGE 16

Answers will vary. Sample answer:

A Great Place to Eat

The Flamboyant Plum is truly a delightful restaurant. I loved it from the first bite to the last. The name of the place comes from the giant painting of a plum in the lobby. "Flamboyant" describes the owner, Miss Alexandra Albright, a woman who dresses in bright purple clothes at all times. She also wears a lot of sequins and other bright things, as well as really high heels.

All of the food and drinks that are served at the Flamboyant Plum are vegetarian, and everything is fresh, well-prepared, and served very attractively on huge square plates with purple flowers painted on them. For appetizers, I especially loved the artichoke dip with olives imported from France. I also loved the plate of crackers and cheese.

When it comes to the main dishes served at the Flamboyant Plum, you can't go wrong. Miss Albright's broccoli quiche is light and tasty, and her goat cheese dumplings are a special treat for anyone who likes goat cheese dumplings (and I do). I first had them on December 26, 2005, at a little place in Albany, New York, and I couldn't believe how good they were. I liked them so much, I ate six servings. All the main dishes are served with a garden salad and your choice of homemade biscuits or homemade blueberry muffins. However, you can also order wheat rolls instead.

For dessert, the choices are amazing. Six different desserts feature chocolate. There are five kinds of fruit pie, several kinds of pudding, and seven flavors of ice cream. I've sampled seven of the desserts, and the chocolate green bean pie is the only one that is not quite wonderful.

Don't delay. Take your family to the Flamboyant Plum this week. You'll be glad you did.

ANSWER KEY

ANSWER KEY

PASSIVE SENTENCES MUST NOT BE WRITTEN BY YOU, PAGE 17

Answers will vary. Sample answers:

1. Joe spilled the tray of gooey cheese nachos all over Mom's new white silk dress.
2. Margaret hid candy bars all over the house.
3. Tony's strange new neighbor devoured sticks of butter.
4. At some time or other, almost all little children eat bugs.
5. Some people consider chocolate covered ants to be delicious.
6. Monkeys eat bananas whole.
7. Bugs are a great source of protein.
8. A giant taco salad he ate for lunch made him sick.
9. Charles filled the plastic wading pool with grape Kool-Aid.
10. The five-year-olds at the birthday party did not like Aunt Alice's broccoli and chocolate tofu shakes.

CRAZY CORNUCOPIA, PAGE 18

Answers will vary. Sample answer:

I drew a Nalgene water bottle as my updated symbol of abundance. The water bottle represents the fantastic outdoor activities that I enjoy year round in sunny Colorado. The bottle is bursting with pictures of snowshoeing, camping, hiking, and cycling. I included a flip-flop as a reminder that the summer is also for relaxing and slowing down (I can't hike or run very well in flip-flops!). I included a laptop computer because we use it to check the weather at the destination of the day. There is also a picture of an ice cream cone from Walrus, my favorite local ice cream shop. My home is pictured because that is where all the abundance in my life starts. Without home, I would not have the energy and encouragement to embrace the world I live in.

WRITE A FOOD AUTOBIOGRAPHY, PAGE 19

Answers will vary. Sample answer:

When I was little, I loved going to the Jack & Jill grocery store with my mom. My favorite thing was the Brach's candy display, a giant pink and white striped carousel divided into sections all the way around like a pie. The display was so tall that I had to stand on tiptoes to see the cellophane wrapped treats.

The Brach's display was simply amazing—all of those different kinds of candy all right there in one place!—but the grocery's own candy display in the checkout line was almost as spectacular and came in at a close second. I drooled over Lemonheads, Boston Baked Beans, Necco Wafers, Bottlecaps, Atomic Fireballs, Circus Peanuts, and candy necklaces. I also liked candy cigarettes, but that is totally politically incorrect now!

My second favorite thing at the grocery store was the soda machine. It had glass bottles of Coke and other kinds of soda, including my favorite, Orange Crush. I'd put my coins in, open the door, and pull out a bottle. And the machine had a bottle opener built right into it so you could open your soda right there!

I guess I really liked sugary treats like soda and candy when I was little because another fond food memory is when we went to the East Coast and I tried rock candy and salt water taffy for the first time. The rock candy was colorful and strange—how did they get it on that stick? And salt water taffy just didn't sound appetizing, but all of the adults were clamoring for another piece, so I had to try it. It was delicious. I liked the surprise of flavors—you couldn't always tell from its colors what a piece would taste like. I liked candy all through my childhood and I still like the sweet, colorful fun it provides.

ANSWER KEY

ANSWER KEY

BITS AND PIECES, PAGE 20

Answers will vary. Sample answers:

1. After picking berries at the farm, I had ripe blueberry stains on my fingers.
2. The triple sausage and cheese pizza was calling my name.
3. Travis was difficult at Thanksgiving dinner, driving his mother crazy by refusing to eat anything that was green.
4. Shari decided to paint a still life of boiled beets in a big blue bowl.
5. There's nothing like a big basket of deep-fried fritters.
6. Pushing the bowl of steamy gruel toward me, the prison guard smirked and said, "Enjoy dinner."
7. I need to stop and buy a package of red licorice whips.
8. We devoured the green bean casserole that Aunt Wanda brought for dinner.
9. The habanero is one of the hottest peppers on earth.
10. I love every vegetable in the universe.
11. The squirrel sat atop the fence, nibbling celery.
12. Because he was shoveling ice cream into his mouth at the birthday party for his friend, Dustin missed singing "Happy Birthday."
13. Celia can't stand the smell of fried onions and garlic.
14. Lee laughed just as he was taking a bite of the beef taco.
15. When the water is boiling, add the pasta.

COPYCATS, PAGE 21

Answers will vary. Sample answer:

To celebrate Mom's birthday last night, we ate at a fancy restaurant called Dominique's Cottage. We did not like it at all. We did not like the snooty waiter, the stuffy atmosphere or the music they played. Also, we did not recognize anything on the menu. My brother and I had to eat chicken cordon bleu because they did not have hamburgers. We did not like it. Because she was smiling at her plate, I knew Mom liked the shrimp scampi she ordered. Dad said that the steak he ordered was delicious. However, he did not like paying the outrageous price for our dinner. My brother, who was always getting into trouble, tipped back his chair. It was no surprise when he fell over. Everyone looked at us, and we really did not like that. The waiter, who was very mad, helped my brother up, but he didn't say anything. We will not be going back.

COOL AS A CUCUMBER, PAGE 22

Answers will vary. Sample answer:

I'm **going bananas**. We are **packed in here like sardines** and my elbows hurt. Holding a company-wide meeting in the break room is a bad idea. Whose **half-baked idea** was this, anyway? I know I'm just a **small fry** around here, but even I know that squeezing 75 people into this room is **recipe for disaster**. Plus, **too many cooks spoil the broth**.

Look at poor Emily Martin. She's **eating for two** and hardly has room to stretch her legs. Jake Hammer, who can **take everything with a grain of salt**, isn't looking like he's having **pie in the sky** daydreams. He's **a bad apple**. Upper-management must be **out to lunch** when it comes to planning meetings. And where are they, anyway? We didn't gather here just to **chew the fat** with our coworkers. The boss acts as if we **just fell off the turnip truck**. They sure do **cook my goose** if I'm more than five minutes late for a meeting. I know that there's **no use crying over spilled milk**, and I've got **bigger fish to fry**, anyway.

Maybe **the big cheese** will storm in here and announce that the company is **raking in the dough** because the new tricycles are **selling like hotcakes**. "It's been like **taking candy from a baby**!" the big cheese will exclaim. Applause will break out and the company will never **play second banana** again. She'll say we are the **cream of the crop** in toy sales and give us all a huge chunk of change to add to our **nest eggs**. Then she'll bring in an incredible catered lunch and we'll all **eat like kings**. Maybe holding this meeting in the break room is a good way to **spice things up**. Of course, that doesn't excuse upper management from being **slow as molasses in January**.

DICTIONARY STEW, PAGE 24

1. | **Spices** | **Cooking Utensils** | **Other** |
   |---|---|---|
   | coriander | colander | columbine |
   | cardamom | cruet | citronella |
   | cumin | carafe | chintz |
   | caraway | | claret |

2. carafe, caraway, cardamom, chintz, cinnamon, citronella, claret, colander, columbine, coriander, cruet, cumin

3. A canapé is an appetizer and a canopy is a cover suspended over a bed. The girl enjoyed a canapé while lying under the canopy.
   A funnel is a utensil and fennel is an herb made of aromatic leaves and seeds. You could pour fennel through a funnel.
   A bushel is a unit of measure, and a bouchée is a small patty shell with creamed filling. I'll put this bouchée in a bushel basket of pastries.

4. You would make tea with bergamot, a type of mint. You would not make tea out of belladonna, a poisonous plant, unless you wanted to stay home from school.

5. You would not serve prosciutto to a vegetarian because it is a type of thinly sliced sausage made from pork.

6. You would eat crudités, or raw vegetables, as an appetizer.

7. Bouillabaisse is a stew made of fish. Bouillon is a clear broth made by straining water in which beef or chicken (usually) has been cooked. Sentence: The chef bought some fish for the bouillabaisse and some meat to make bouillon.

8. She threw a dash of salt into the soup before she had to dash out to the store.
   Instead of rolling the dice, you must dice up the onions.
   Hand me a pinch of salt before I pinch you.

9. Fondant does not belong because it is used in desserts, while all the others are types of meat stew.

10. bake, barbeque, baste, beat, blacken, blanch, blend, boil, braise, brew, broil

ANSWER KEY

MORE DICTIONARY STEW, PAGE 25

Answers will vary. Sample answers:

1. When Sally served the freshly baked French baguette that was the color of a charcoal briquette, the dinner guests fell into a regretful silence.
2. While munching on cinnamon toast, Uncle Felix said that the cinnabar shirt I picked out for picture day reminded him of a speeding fire truck.
3. They mean that it tastes great.
4. You scald them briefly in boiling water.
5. Megan was horrified when her dad showed up with a hosta plant instead of pasta at the pre-track meet carbohydrate party.
6. Sheridan's Sultry Strawberry Rhubarb pie has a delightfully piquant taste that is sure to linger in the minds of all who experience it.
7. The pullet ran from the butcher, who in turn ran from the artist and his palette, but all three thought about the dinner that would please the palate later that night.
8. Canned peas are so disgusting that the the Food and Drug Administration should ban them and mothers and father should never, ever cook them.
9. Each small dish held a large amount of juicy berries, thinly sliced bananas, and a splash of cream.
10. cappuccino, cocoa, coffee, espresso, iced tea, java, juice, lemonade, malt, milk, milk shake, punch, root beer, soda, sparkling water, spritzer, tea, tonic, water.

KEY INGREDIENTS, PAGE 26

Answers will vary. Sample answers:

1. (no adjectives except a, an, the) Yesterday, I went to Food Heaven with Zeke. We ate pizza, chicken, cookies, and ice cream. We enjoyed it.
2. (no pronouns) When Clara was eating at Food Heaven last night, Clara saw Mrs. Smith and Mrs. Smith's daughter, Angie. Mrs. Smith and Angie were eating nachos and drinking sodas. Mrs. Smith was smiling at Angie and asking Angie questions about the new play Angie was in. Angie was picked to play the role of Belle in the school's production of *Beauty and the Beast.* Mrs. Smith was thrilled that Angie was chosen for the lead role. Angie was thrilled, too. Angie was also happy that Joe was playing the Beast. Angie thought Joe was cute.
3. (no prepositions) The family was hungry. They chose Food Heaven. They were seated, reading menus. Dad ordered steak, Mom ordered fish, and the twin girls ordered macaroni and cheese. When the food came, they all started devouring their meals. They were really hungry.
4. (no conjuctions) The couple was very picky. I was very attentive. Their food was fresh, hot. They wanted something else. I told the chef to make it. They didn't like it. I asked another server, Adam, to recommend something to the couple. He did. The chef made it. They hated it. We tried everything. We even gave them free dessert. They weren't impressed.

ANSWER KEY

COFFEE OR A ROLLER COASTER, PAGE 27

Answers will vary. Sample answers:

1. A smile weighs less than a brownie because it has no calories. A brownie, however, is loaded with them.
2. Broccoli and a cell phone both have a double consonant.
3. Bread is a staple, and a stapler uses staples.
4. A baseball cap is happier than a pepperoni pizza because it's on top where it can see the game. A pizza just winds up in a dark stomach.
5. A bowl of oatmeal is lonelier than a hangnail because it doesn't have anyone to "hang" around with.
6. A salad is crazier than an eyebrow because it has been tossed and gotten all mixed up.
7. Spaghetti and a motorcycle both go fast.
8. A marshmallow is funnier than a fork. Who laughs at something that stabs meat?
9. A butterfly is stronger than strawberry jelly because it lifts itself into the air. Jelly just sits there.
10. You squeeze both an accordion and a tube of toothpaste.

CAFETERIA, PAGE 28

Part A.
1. eat
2. feta
3. tea
4. cater
5. fat
6. feet
7. café
8. carafe
9. rice
10. ice

Part B.   Answers will vary on the next section. Sample answers:

1. Something that is true is a <u>fact</u>.
2. People sometimes shed a <u>tear</u> at a sad movie.
3. Something to sit by when you go camping: <u>fire</u>
4. A soft, cuddly pet known for its independence is a <u>cat</u>.
5. Huck Finn & Tom Sawyer floated down the river on a <u>raft</u>.
6. It's not good when one of these is flat: <u>tire</u>.
7. When your clothes are the right size, they <u>fit</u>.
8. Something people feel when danger is near: <u>fear</u>
9. A painting is referred to as a work of <u>art</u>.
10. When you cross the finish line first, you win the <u>race</u>.

ANSWER KEY

ANSWER KEY

CHEESY RHYMES, PAGE 29

Answers will vary. Sample answers:

I like cheese, sharp or mellow.
I like cheese, white or yellow.
I like cheese that's hard or runny,
and cheese that costs a lot of money.
I like cheese, Brie or cheddar,
but mozzarella's even better.

Shakespearean Sonnet:

This thing called cheese I love and eat with glee,
I do not care that it is made with mold.
From cheddar up to Parmesan and Brie.
They all are worth ten times their weight in gold.
I never wonder, should I laugh or cry
Over pounds I've gained from my obsession.
For if I were to stop, I'd surely die
Or slip into a serious depression.
Cheese will forever be my favorite thing,
Be it Gouda, feta, Monterey Jack.
Any kind of cheese will make my heart sing
Because it really is the perfect snack.
Give me cheese any time of day or night.
For eating cheese will always make things right.

OLIVIA'S CAFE, PAGE 30

Answers will vary. Sample answers:

Details chosen to show that it is a healthy, nutritious place to eat: Olivia's Café is a restaurant that serves sandwiches made from whole grain breads and organic produce grown locally with no pesticides. People love the smoothies, which are made with fresh fruit. If you are worried about kids having too much sugar, come here. Nothing has added sugar; everything is sweetened naturally. No trans fats are used in the cooking, and special menus are available for diabetics or people with wheat allergies.

Details chosen to show that it has a friendly, inviting atmosphere: Open the door to Olivia's Cafe, and the cheerful yellow walls invite you right in. Order a smoothie, and it will be served in a red tumbler decorated with rainbows. Your food will come artfully arranged on colorful red plates. Sunshine streams through the windows, and the tables with fresh flowers in the center are arranged in friendly little groupings. Kids come in on dates. Ladies lunch there. People often sit and linger over coffee because it is so pleasant there.

ANSWER KEY

OVERSTUFFED SENTENCES, PAGE 31

1. The beef burgundy made my nose twitch.
2. The bowl was filled with beans.
3. Most food will taste better if you add fragrant garlic.
4. She ate too much at the buffet and threw up.
5. Although he wasn't hungry, he ate five bowls of pasta.
6. You really know how to cook on the grill.
7. I admire anyone who can make a good loaf of bread.
8. Stop being picky about your food and try something new.
9. If I had a dollar for every time someone asked me, "Do you want fries with that," I'd be rich.
10. Where's the dessert?

IN COMMON...OR NOT, PAGE 32

Answers will vary. Sample answers:

1. All are red.
2. All are often eaten from a bowl.
3. All are served hot.
4. All are made of multiple ingredients.
5. All are round.
6. All have double consonants, except for beef.
7. All can be boiled, except for cake.
8. All end in vowels, except for pear.

Bonus. In common:
1. Potato chips, candy bars, bananas, donuts (All can be eaten without silverware.)
2. Saltine crackers, sandwich bread, ravioli, individually-wrapped cheese slices (All are square.)
3. Broccoli, asparagus, lime, moldy bread, lettuce (All are green.)

SENTIMENTAL JOURNEY, PAGE 33

Answers will vary. Sample answer:

My aunt Mary is the oldest in a family of nine kids. Nine kids! Not surprisingly, they didn't eat out that much because her parents couldn't afford to take all those kids out to dinner. When they did go out, usually for Mexican food, it was a big deal. Growing up in Colorado, Aunt Mary says Mexican food was very plentiful, very authentic, and very good. Their family members from the East Coast thought Mexican food was exotic, but to them it was very familiar. She said there was no such thing as cheap fast food back then, until the first fast food place opened—a McDonald's—in her neighborhood. They didn't go there a lot, though. Besides, she says, her mom's cooking was much better.

In her family, Aunt Mary's mom did most of the cooking, along with help from the older kids. Because she was the oldest, she learned to cook at a young age. All of the kids in the family had to help out with the meals because their mom couldn't handle cooking for all those people. She remembers her mom making the kids eat peanut butter, mayonnaise, and lettuce sandwiches. She packed them in their school lunches, even though they hated them. Aunt Mary preferred peanut butter and jelly sandwiches.

Her family had common food traditions, such as turkey at Thanksgiving and Christmas and ham at Easter, but she says their family also prepared some special meals. Her mom made scrapple, which is a sort of meat loaf made from the scraps of pork roast mixed with cornmeal, flour, and seasoning. After forming the loaf, you slice it into pieces and fry it up. She says her mom, who is Irish, also made Irish soda bread and corned beef and cabbage on St. Patrick's Day. Sometimes they would make goulash on special occasions. They also made homemade peach ice cream on the Fourth of July. She remembers the younger kids would have to sit on the lid of the old fashioned ice cream maker to hold it down—they didn't have electric ice cream makers back then—and the older kids would take turns putting ice and salt in the maker and turning the crank. She said it took forever to make ice cream this way. Kids would be out on the porch all day long, taking turns cranking the ice and salt in the ice cream maker. The wonderful results made it all worth it, though.

DELICIOUS AND DISGUSTING, PAGE 34
Answers will vary. Sample answers:

Delicious: I stood there staring, my mouth watering at what the shallow clear glass dish contained. On top of three cold white scoops, three tempting liquids were drizzled. One was a refreshing yellow. One was a sticky-sweet red. One was a sweet, brown concoction that is popular on Valentine's Day. The entire delicious mess was bordered by two slices of a yellow thing that grows in bunches. (a banana split)

Disgusting: I groaned when I saw the jar on the counter. Mom was pulling out the slimy green slices of a common garden item floating in the murky brine. Each slice had prickly little bumps around the edge, and I knew from past experience about the sour taste. I did *not* want these slices on my hamburger. When would my mother ever learn? (pickle slices)

APPETIZING ANTONYMS, PAGE 35

1. s
2. c
3. d
4. n
5. m
6. k
7. p
8. j
9. o
10. g
11. e
12. l
13. r
14. a
15. q
16. t

17. h
18. f
19. i
20. b

Answers will vary for the next section. Sample answers:

Option 1 (20 sentences)
1. You don't usually get **bad** food at a **good** restaurant.
2. In winter, I enjoy **hot** chocolate, but I prefer **cold** drinks in the summer.
3. When food is hot and **spicy**, it's nice to have a **bland** side dish to tone it down.
4. Squirrels may like **crunchy** peanut butter, but I prefer the **creamy** variety.
5. **Raw** eggs taste pretty good in cookie dough, but for breakfast, they need to be **cooked**.
6. A **sweet** strawberry tastes a whole lot better than a **sour** lemon, in my opinion.
7. **Flavorful** home-cooked meals are far more appetizing than **tasteless**, prepackaged food from 7-11.
8. **Fresh** milk must be refrigerated in order to keep it from getting **spoiled**.
9. Nutritionists recommend that **frozen** meat be **thawed** in the refrigerator instead of at room temperature.
10. When making cookie dough, you blend the **wet** ingredients together before adding the **dry** ingredients.
11. Most egg recipes instruct you to **blend** the egg yolks and egg whites together, but if you're making lemon meringue pie, you have to **separate** them.
12. Your hamburger will be easier to handle if you use **thick** ketchup on it instead of the cheap, **runny** stuff.
13. A **crisp** slice of toast will get **soggy** in a hurry if you put too much butter and jelly on it.
14. The **smooth** pancake batter was pretty **lumpy** before I dumped it into the blender.
15. I prefer my chocolate to be **solid**, but I've actually seen advertisements for a **liquid** chocolate fountain.
16. French bread has a **hard** crust, but it's **soft** inside.
17. **Dark** bread has more fiber, is more flavorful, and is healthier to eat than **light** bread that has had most of the fiber and nutrients removed.
18. **Strong** coffee will perk you up in the morning, but if you want to sleep at night, try a **weak** cup of chamomile tea instead.
19. **Warm** bread, fresh from the oven, is a delightful treat, but it still tastes good when it's **cool**.
20. Flank steak is a **chewy** cut of meat unless you use a marinade to make it **tender**.

FOOD TO WRITE HOME ABOUT, PAGE 36

Answers will vary. Sample answers:

1. My comfort food is hot chocolate with marshmallows. A steaming cup of it reminds me of being safe and warm inside on a cold winter day. Mom used to make hot chocolate with marshmallows for my brother and me when we were little, after we'd come in from playing outside in the snow. Our faces would be all red from the cold, and our fingers nearly frozen. Then she would hand us steaming cups and we would warm right up. She would just load the cup with marshmallows because she knew that we liked them even more than the hot chocolate.

2. The number one food that really disgusts me is poached eggs. Just the thought of eating those slimy yellow yolks and those runny egg whites is enough to make me gag. When I go out for breakfast with friends and they order poached eggs, I have to prop up a menu between us so I don't have to look. Otherwise, I can't eat my own breakfast. When we go to Aunt Kate's house for Christmas brunch, she always makes poached eggs with hollandaise sauce for everyone but my mom and me. For us, she scrambles the eggs, *hard*. I know my hatred of poached eggs comes from my mom. She hates them, and her hatred must have passed on to me. I guess my brother got more of my dad's genes. They both *love* poached eggs. Of course, Dad has to be the one to cook them, not Mom or me!

REALISM SQUAD, PAGE 37

Answers will vary. Sample answers:

1. The lunch special that's causing you to drool is a dead bird covered in stale pulverized bread, marginally cooked and camouflaged with tiny strips of overcooked, chemically preserved dead pig and a warm stringy product made from the coagulated lumps of spoiled cow's milk, laid out on bread made from soured milk, probably also from a cow. This is brought out with a mixture of milk fat and squashed tomatoes made from an old recipe that belonged to the restaurant owner's great-grandmother.

2. All the people in your family who eat like pigs will look like smiling pigs after eating at Gargantuoso. At Gargantuoso, we know that pigs can never have too much to eat. Everything we serve comes with the same thing: an artery-clogging pile of processed white vegetables grown underground, processed and formed into long uniform strips that are soaked and deep-fried in synthetic fat. Dinner also comes with an endless supply of water with carbon injected into it and mixed with artificially flavored high calorie liquid sugar. Each meal ends with a slab of a dark colored baked product made from bleached ground wheat, ground cocoa beans, processed sweetener, solidified milk fat and the egg of a chicken. This is covered with frozen, artificially flavored milk fat and a thick liquid made from concentrated ground cocoa beans, milk fat, and an unknown substance.

DINNER CONVERSATION, PAGE 38

Answers will vary. Sample answer:

"Dad said I could go to the movies tomorrow with Kevin," Sarah said, while slurping up a piece of spaghetti.

"Excuse me?" her mom said, throwing a glance at Dad.

"Dad said I could go to the movies tomorrow."

"Oh, really?" Mom pushed her asparagus to the edge of her plate and decided to take a few deep breaths before proceeding. "On a school night?"

"Sarah, I said you had to talk to your mom to see if it was okay with her," Dad reminded Sarah.

"Yeah, but you said I could go." She slurped again.

Mom sat with her hands in her lap and her eyes on Dad. She was not happy.

"I said you could go if it was okay with Mom," he said. He glanced at his wife and quickly dunked his bread into the garlic, cheese, and olive oil dip. He crammed the soggy bread into his mouth and said, "Wow, this is good stuff. I'm glad we came here."

"Don't talk with your mouth full, Charlie." Mom shook her head in annoyance and turned to Sarah. "Is Dad going to the movie with you?"

"What do you mean, 'Is Dad going?' You're funny, Mom." Sarah tried to remain cool, but the thought of showing up at the movie theater with her dad was mortifying.

"And who are you going with? Did I hear a boy's name? Kevin?" Mom took a bite of her salad.

"Yeah, Kevin. I've told you about him. He's in my algebra class. He plays soccer."

"Oh, right, soccer. Kevin and Dad will have so much to talk about because they both love soccer." Sarah swallowed some soda and started to get really nervous.

"Sarah, you may go to the movies, but Dad needs to chaperone. Now, does anybody care for dessert?" She smiled. "You know, this really is a great place to eat."

IT'S ALL IN YOUR POINT OF VIEW, PAGE 39

Answers will vary. Sample answers:

1. Little Savanna yelled, "I want the burger with the toy! From McDonald's! I want to play with the other kids there. Can we go? Can we go? Can we go?"
2. She stared at the greasy gray patty lying on the bun, and all she could think was "dead cow." Then she imagined sweet, brown-eyed Freida, the cow on her grandpa's farm, and she burst into tears. "How could anyone put someone like Freida on a bun?" she sobbed.
3. He took his spatula and carefully slid it under the last patty on the grill. This one would top his tower of perfect patties. The last patty was perfectly round, juicy and thick, and had ideal black grill marks across it in a neat row. It was like a picture from a magazine. He smiled proudly.
4. "If I never see another hamburger in my life, it will be too soon," thought Frank, scowling as he scrubbed his hands. No matter how hard he tried, he always smelled vaguely like onion. Watching those patties sizzle and spurt in grease on the grill had made him become a real fan of fish. Fresh fish. Broiled.

SUPER-SIZED FOOD CHALLENGE, PAGES 40-45

1. Four and twenty
2. *Through the Looking-Glass*
3. Nutria are large, semi-aquatic rodents.
4. False.
5. Haggis is a traditional Scottish dish made with a sheep's heart, liver, and lungs, minced with onions, oatmeal, and spices, and then boiled in the sheep's stomach.
6. chestnuts
7. India
8. Fugu is dangerous because it's a poisonous pufferfish.
9. cabbage
10. hot, spicy, fresh, wrapped, seasoned
11. *A Christmas Carol*
12. 16
13. cat, late, eat, hat, hole, ate, tea, teal, hate, cocoa, coal, hoot, cola, loot, each, chat, tale, tool, latch, ace
14. peanuts and Cracker Jack
15. adjective
16. wok

17. red, read, bed, led, lead, wed, fled, dead, dread, said, stead, fed, head, tread, zed
18. Answers will vary. Sample: They're there at the buffet, filling their plates.
19. Leo
20. George Crum
21. California
22. bologna
23. United States Department of Agriculture
24. grub, chow, fare, provisions, victuals
25. Arthur Wellesley, the first Duke of Wellington
26. False.
27. ax, fax, facts, hacks, jacks, lax, lacks, packs, quacks, racks, sacks, sax, tax, tacks, wax
28. Entomophagy is the practice of eating insects as a food source.
29. carnation, chrysanthemum, fuchsia, gardenia, gladiolus, hibiscus, lilac, marigold, pansy, peony
30. Red Hot Chili Peppers, Bread, Meat loaf, Cake, Smashing Pumpkins, The Cranberries, Ice T, Black Eyed Peas, The Electric Prunes, Tangerine Dream
31. an edible starchy root of a legume
32. Ruth Reichl. Subtitle – Growing Up at the Table
33. movie
34. Wisconsin
35. Julia Child
36. Answers will vary. Sample: If I had eaten all of those potato chips...
37. *Peanuts*
38. Answers will vary. Sample:
    Call it a vice, but
    I love rice.
    It's so nice.
    I'll eat it twice.
39. Belgium
40. orange
41. basil, oregano, parsley, tarragon, thyme, sage, rosemary, dill, cilantro, fennel
42. pudding
43. derby pie
44. boysenberry, raspberry, blueberry, blackberry, strawberry, lingonberry, cranberry, gooseberry, mulberry, huckleberry
45. Eggroll
46. salt of the earth, apple of my eye, cream of the crop, just my cup of tea, flat as a pancake, nutty as a fruitcake, butter him up, bring home the bacon, easy as pie, spill the beans
47. salt and pepper, peaches and cream, meat and potatoes, toast and jam, fish and chips, chips and salsa, cake and ice cream, turkey and dressing, cheese and crackers, peanut butter and jelly
48. fruit of an Asian tree, resembles an apple
49. chocolate
50. Wendy's TV commercial

51. Ben and Jerry
52. someone who eats no meat or food containing animal products
53. bread
54. Olive Oyl
55. Answers will vary. Samples: "Banana Boat Song," "The Candy Man," "Brown Sugar, "Found a Peanut," "Lemon Tree."
56. *Breakfast at Tiffany's*
57. vegetable
58. raisins, raspberries, ribs, ravioli, rutabaga
59. Sample: I said "please" when I politely prompted Paula to pass the pumpkin pie and the pitcher of pomegranate juice.
60. Pisces
61. chicken, chocolate, coffee, cheese, cucumbers, corn, candy, cake, carrots, celery
62. A roux is a cooked mixture of flour and fat, used to thicken soup or sauce.
63. saffron
64. goat's milk or sheep's milk
65. a seed or a grain, depending on who you ask
66. cottage cheese
67. biscuits
68. hors d'oeuvres
69. Washington Huskies
70. Only one group in class can complete this item.
71. salmon, salsa, sauce, Snapple, Snickers, soup, soy sauce, Spam, spinach
72. I never saw a purple cow,
    I never hope to see one;
    But I can tell you this right now:
    I'd rather see than be one.

    Ah, yes, I wrote "The Purple Cow"—
    I'm sorry now I wrote it.
    But I can tell you anyhow,
    I'll kill you if you quote it.
73. *The Lorax, If I Ran the Zoo, The Cat in the Hat, Horton Hears a Who!, Yurtle the Turtle* (and others)
74. The potato's eyes stared at me.
75. donut, meat, beet, eggplant, apricot, grapefruit, halibut, peppermint, wheat, peanut, walnut, eggs benedict, fish filet, biscuit, trout, toast, omelet, salt, carrot, fruit.

RACE OF TENS #1, PAGE 46

Answers will vary. Sample answers:

1. cucumber, corn, celery, spinach, turnip, green pepper, zucchini, carrot, broccoli, cauliflower
2. lettuce, cabbage, tangerine, orange, apple, chocolate, pie, applesauce, cheese, pineapple
3. boil, slice, dice, cut, fry, coat, soak, thaw, sauté, roast

4. How long should I **boil** the potatoes?
Please **slice** these tomatoes for the salad.
Dice the onions for the tacos.
Cut the squash into small pieces before you cook it.
Fry the fish in oil after you **coat** it in flour.
Soak the beans before cooking, or they will be hard.
Thaw out the chicken before you try to stuff it.
Sauté the vegetables in olive oil, and then add them to the roast.
Roast the corn in its husks for the best taste.
5. soda, water, milk, hot tea, iced tea, hot cider, coffee, juice, lemonade, milkshake
6. cherry, tomato, strawberry, beet, radish, red licorice, red pepper, chili, pimento, cranberry
7. grapefruit, onion, cantaloupe, plum, grapes, blueberry, peach, pea, olive, nectarine
8. radish, papaya, banana, hot dog, coffee, squash, turkey, pepper, cookie, pickle
9. lasagna, ravioli, apricot, coconut, avocado, pumpkin, sausage, chicken, oatmeal, custard
10. My grandma makes the best spaghetti in the whole world.

RACE OF TENS #2, PAGE 47

Answers will vary. Sample answers:

1. lemon, lime, sour cream, sauerkraut, green grapes, green apple, sour cherry, pickle, vinegar, sour gummy candy
2. orange, pear, plum, apricot, peach, fig, papaya, mango, guava, persimmon
3. avocado, cake, eggs, gravy, ice cream, ketchup, macaroni, onion, quince, spaghetti, upside-down cake, watermelon, yams
4. I love the taste of fresh **avocado**.
Please hand her another piece of **cake**.
We always have scrambled **eggs** for breakfast.
My brother loves **gravy** on his french fries.
He decided to cut back on his consumption of **ice cream**.
Frank won't eat a hot dog without **ketchup**.
My favorite comfort food is **macaroni** and cheese.
Melissa wants a little more **onion** on her salad.
Have you ever eaten a **quince**?
The Italian buffet is out of **spaghetti**.
We had **upside-down** cake at Grandma's house.
If you buy **watermelon**, get the seedless kind.
Her sister hates **yams**.
5. at, can, cans, cap, caps, car, carp, cars, cart, carts, cat, cats, dam, dams, dart, darts, dump, dumps, dust, dusts, mad, man, map, maps, mass, mast, masts, mat, mats, must, nap, naps, pad, pads, pan, panda, pandas, pans, par, pass, past, pat, pats, pus, put, puts, putt, putts, part, parts, ram, rams, ran, rat, rats, run, runs, rust, rusts, rut, ruts, sad, sand, sands, sap, saps, sat, scam, scams, scan, scans, scar, scars, spat, spud, spuds, stamp, stamps, star, stars, start, starts, stump, stumps, sum, sums, sun, suns, tad, tamp, tamps, tan, tans, tap, taps, tar, tars, tart, tarts, up

6.   garlic, ginger, grain, granola, grape, grapefruit, gravy, guava, gum, gumbo
7.   salt, pepper, nutmeg, sage, thyme, cayenne, cinnamon, paprika, oregano, rosemary
8.   door, girl, station, carpet, store, fork, newspaper, spider, nose, pencil
9.   The door slammed when Sarah angrily left the room with the pizza.
     The girl gobbled up the lobster.
     The train station was packed with children holding popsicles.
     The popsicle melted all over the white carpet.
     Another new candy store is going in at the corner.
     He stabbed the hot dog with his fork.
     The newspaper crashed through the front window and landed in my cereal.
     The spider crawled onto the chocolate cake.
     His nose told him that something good was simmering on the stove.
     Since she didn't have a toothpick, she used a pencil to see if the cake was done.
10. I skipped happily along the path to the candy store,
     What I didn't know was the store wasn't there anymore.

STORY STARTERS, PAGE 48
Answers will vary. Sample answer:

   "The soup of the day is cream of termite," said the waitress. She stared at Mr. Harcourt, daring him with her eyes to say something. Every day he complained. Every day he criticized. Every day he drove her crazy. She decided that today she would give him something to complain about. "Would you like a bowl?" she asked innocently, stepping on his foot "accidentally" and handing him a water glass with lipstick prints on the edge. She took out her pen to take his order and smiled.

METAPHORS AND SIMILES, PAGE 49
Answers will vary. Sample answers:

1.   Gertrude's face was as red as a beet and her cotton candy hair stood out in all directions. Sweat poured off of her green bean-like figure—so thin, so stringy.
2.   Mom combed Baby Jenny's hair, which was as soft as peach fuzz. Jenny's strawberry lips pouted sweetly as she squirmed, trying to get away from the hair brush. "You're my fidgety little sweet potato, aren't you," said Mom.
3.   Mort's body was shaped like a boiled egg and his jelly belly jiggled when he walked. His hair was as black as molasses and his cauliflower nose twitched when he talked.

SATISFYINGLY SWEET AND SAVORY, PAGE 50
Answers will vary. Sample answer:

   Steve and Sandy went out for Sunday night supper at Sam's Southwest Salsa Station. They sat in a secluded booth with soft striped cushions. A silly song was playing on the stereo. Sandy started her meal by sipping a spicy soup while Steve slurped a strawberry soda. They searched the selections on the menu for a single meal to split. Since it was a southwest style restaurant, steak and seafood weren't available, so they selected the special of the day, the "sizzling sombrero skillet" made with sausage and Spanish rice and served with a side salad topped with tortilla strips. The house dressing was a simple blend of salsa and sour cream. They savored the superb and satisfying flavors of their selection. Their server stayed nearby, making sure to supply Steve and Sandy with seconds on their sodas. Suddenly, a strikingly beautiful singer started strolling around with a stringed instrument, serenading several of the senior citizens seated in the restaurant. Steve smiled and Sandy sighed, seemingly smitten by the sweet sound of the singing.

Soon it was time to see if there was some kind of dessert they could share. They decided to splurge and have sugar coated sopapillas slathered with honey flavored syrup. They slowly ate their rather sloppy dessert, surprised that they were still able to stuff in one more bite. Surely their stomachs wouldn't show any sign of swelling after their sumptuous feast. They swore that they would start having smaller servings someday. They settled their tab and stretched before standing up from their seats. They said "thank you" to their server and strode out of the restaurant, stopping to stroke a stray kitten sitting on the sidewalk outside. They scooped up the kitten, got into their sporty new Saturn and headed out to search for a store that sold pet supplies. Their Sunday night had been simply sensational. (Score: 124)

FOOD CHAIN, PAGE 51

1.	ice cream	27.	apple	53.	navy bean	77.	saltines
2.	mustard	28.	escargot	54.	noodles	78.	scallops
3.	dressing	29.	tomato	55.	salami	79.	shark
4.	grapefruit	30.	octopus	56.	Irish soda bread	80.	ketchup
5.	tangerine	31.	sardines			81.	pancake
6.	egg roll	32.	shrimp	57.	duck	82.	endive
7.	lemon	33.	pizza	58.	kale	83.	empanada
8.	nutmeg	34.	avocado	59.	English muffin	84.	antipasto
9.	ginger	35.	okra	60.	nachos	85.	olive oil
10.	relish	36.	artichokes	61.	syrup	86.	leeks
11.	hot dog	37.	spaghetti	62.	peas	87.	spinach
12.	granola	38.	icing	63.	succotash	88.	hamburger
13.	asparagus	39.	grapes	64.	haggis	89.	romaine
14.	soup	40.	squash	65.	sandwich	90.	eggs
15.	potato	41.	honey	66.	halibut	91.	string beans
16.	oregano	42.	yogurt	67.	taffy	92.	sugar
17.	orange	43.	tofu	68.	Yankee pot roast	93.	radish
18.	eggplant	44.	unagi			94.	ham
19.	turkey	45.	instant oatmeal	69.	tortellini	95.	mushrooms
20.	yam	46.	lamb	70.	Indian corn	96.	strawberries
21.	milk	47.	bread	71.	nougat	97.	sweet potatoes
22.	kiwi	48.	dark chocolate	72.	truffles	98.	soybeans
23.	iceberg lettuce	49.	éclair	73.	sherbet	99.	squid
24.	enchilada	50.	rutabaga	74.	tabbouleh	100.	dill
25.	apricot	51.	alligator	75.	habanero		
26.	tuna	52.	raisin	76.	olives		

ANSWER KEY

FOOD SCRAMBLE, PAGE 52

1. hamburger
2. coconut
3. lasagna
4. provolone
5. spinach
6. pizza
7. guacamole
8. cinnamon
9. pancakes
10. squash
11. hot dog
12. pumpernickel
13. asparagus
14. waffles
15. broccoli
16. banana
17. prime rib
18. bacon
19. artichoke
20. spaghetti
21. pepperoni
22. cantaloupe
23. marshmallow
24. sushi
25. avocado
26. casserole
27. tomato
28. watermelon
29. portobello
30. brussels sprouts
31. mushroom
32. quesadilla
33. macaroni
34. sausage
35. green beans
36. pork chop
37. meat loaf
38. potatoes
39. meatballs
40. corn bread
41. tortellini
42. teriyaki
43. eggplant
44. burrito
45. papaya
46. mango
47. enchilada
48. lemonade
49. bagel
50. chicken

SOMETHING FISHY'S GOING ON, PAGE 53

Answers will vary. Sample answer:

Megan knew she loved Sly with her **heart and sole**. Her heart raced whenever he walked by. Then one day, Megan decided to approach Sly and talk to him. He seemed to be having a **whale of time** working out with his friends, but that didn't interfere with Megan's plans. She **perched** on an exercise bike next to Sly's weight machine.

"**Put some mussel behind it**!" she yelled. She wasn't tongue-**tide** at all. Sly stared at her.

"Who are you to give me advice?" he asked.

"I'm just someone who has been **herring** about how strong you are. I'd like to see it."

"Something **fishy** is going on," Sly said. "Nobody talks about how strong I am. I'm not."

"Okay, you're not. I just wanted to talk to you, " said Megan. I am **o-fish-ally** asking you on a date.

"Okay, when?" Sly said.

"Friday," said Megan. She thought, "He doesn't seem **super-fish-al** at all," and she **reeled** him in. That's **a moray!**

SENTENCE COMBINING, PAGE 54

Answers will vary. Sample answers:

1. Victor was extremely hungry at lunchtime, so he went to the school cafeteria to see what was for lunch. The brownish food being scooped into trays resembled meat, but he wasn't sure it was even food. He was sure of one thing—it didn't look good. He settled instead for a squashed granola bar he found in his backpack.

ANSWER KEY

1b. By lunchtime, Victor was extremely hungry and went to the school cafeteria to see what was being served. The food being scooped into trays resembled brown meat, but he wasn't sure it was even food. He was sure that he didn't want any. He decided to eat the squashed granola bar in his backpack. It would probably taste better than the brownish food.

2. Allie was babysitting two-year-old Tyrone, who has the nickname Terrible Tyrone. She was trying to feed him peas, which he doesn't like. He also doesn't like babysitters, so he spit the peas clear across the room. Some of them landed in Allie's hair, and she was mad. She had a date later with Calvin, a guy she really likes. She doesn't like Terrible Tyrone very much.

2b. When Allie, the babysitter, tried to feed two-year-old Tyrone some peas, he spit them clear across the room. He doesn't like peas. He also doesn't like Allie. She doesn't like Terrible Tyrone, either. She was mad because she had a date later with Calvin, a guy she really likes. But now she had peas in her hair.

DISHING UP THE INTERNET, PAGE 55

1. Aubergine is found in a garden. Abalone is found in the ocean. Agave is found in the desert.
2. They are all deep-fried.
3. It comes from the belly muscles of a cow.
4. A jambon does not contain jam. *Jambon* is French for *ham,* and ham does not come from a cow.
5. The main ingredient in p'tcha is calves' feet or hooves.
6. After we enjoyed the garbure, our host brought out a beautiful ganache cake garnished with fresh mint leaves.
7. Pappardelle doesn't belong in the list because it is a kind of pasta, and the other names in the list are kinds of soup.
8. Julia Child. *The Way to Cook.* (There are others, as well.)
9. Quick breads don't use use yeast for leavening, as regular breads do. They use chemical leaveners like baking powder.
10. Lard is pig fat. It is used in soaps.

WHERE'S THE FOOD?, PAGE 56

1. I'm impressed that Bo**B READ** the entire book to Ben**JAM**in.
2. Meet **ME AT** 10:00 in front of the train de**POT AT OES**terfield and 42nd Avenue.
3. I asked the ric**H AM**erican tourist if she could may**BE ANS**wer my question.
4. I ho**PE A CHES**tnut tree will grow in my one a**CRE, AM**azingly beautiful garden.
5. George went to **TO A ST**treet dance, **BUT TER**RY decided to go the library.

Answers will vary on the next section. Sample answers:

1. As soon as you start to **COOK, I E**xpect MaC **AND Y**vonne to show up.
2. Before you take a n**AP, PLE**ase put that **PIE**ce of glass away.
3. Susan walke**D IN NER**vously and looked doubtfully at the ol**D RINK** before putting on her ice skates.

ANSWER KEY

YOU ARE HOW YOU EAT, PAGE 57

Answers will vary. Sample answer:

Marion and her ten-year-old daughter Riley sat across from each other in the restaurant's only corner booth. After they ordered lunch, Riley asked her mother again, and, again, Marion shook her head "no." Riley rolled her eyes, but Marion just smiled at the waiter delivering the food. "This looks delicious," she said, digging into her ravioli. Riley slammed her fork on the table and folded her arms across her chest, frowning and glaring at her plate of spaghetti. Marion shrugged and kept on eating.

VERBING YOUR FOOD, PAGE 58

Answers will vary. Sample answers:

1. Oil: You need to oil the pan. I don't like too much oil in my salad dressing.
2. Peel: Will you please peel the potatoes? Grate the orange peel.
3. Slurp: Don't slurp your soup. He took a big slurp of eggnog.
4. Chew: She chewed the bubblegum. They fought over the last ginger chew.
5. Grill: We grilled the chicken. Dad wouldn't let anyone near the grill.
6. Roll: Roll the donut holes in sugar. I would like a dinner roll.
7. Boil: They forgot to boil the vegetables. My sister has a nasty boil on her leg.
8. Microwave: I need to microwave a potato. Let's move the microwave.
9. Thaw: Leave the hamburger out to thaw. We'll dig up the garden beds after the first thaw.
10. Season: I like to season my French fries with garlic salt. My favorite season is summer.

For a bigger challenge:
1. Roast: The roast was roasted in the oven.
2. Slice: I started slicing off a slice of meat loaf.
3. Scramble: The kids would always scramble to the kitchen table to enjoy potato, bacon, and egg scramble.
4. Melt: The cheese didn't melt on my tuna melt.
5. Mix: We decided to mix the ingredients in the brownie mix.

ALEX HATED IT, PAGE 59

Answers will vary. Sample answers:

Alex hated it:
1. Alex vigorously protested the presence of brussels sprouts on his dinner plate.
2. The smell of boiled brussels sprouts drove Alex out of the house, screaming.
3. When he saw the brussels sprouts, Alex clutched his stomach and fell on the floor, making retching noises.
4. The cooked brussels sprouts sent Alex into a downward spiral of depression.
5. Alex's parents said he had to sit at the dinner table and finish his dinner when they had brussels sprouts. He sat for a very, very, very long time before they finally gave in.
6. If brussels sprouts are on the menu, Alex will throw a nasty temper tantrum.

7. Alex always chucks his brussels sprouts across the room and into the wastebasket when no one is looking.
8. Alex smashes up his brussels sprouts, puts them in a napkin, and slips them to the cat.
9. When Alex's mom tells him they are having brussels sprouts with dinner, he asks if he can visit his cousins.
10. Alex pretends to wipe his mouth, but he's really spitting his brussels sprouts into his napkin.

Alex served it:
1. Feeling generous, Alex plopped extra helpings of peach cobbler on the students' trays.
2. Alex scooped peach cobbler into the awaiting bowls.
3. Alex portioned out the peach cobbler so that everyone got an equal amount.
4. Alex slipped some peach cobbler onto each plate.
5. Alex dumped peach cobbler into each bowl.
6. Alex divided the peach cobbler equally among the students.
7. Alex doled out the peach cobbler.
8. Reluctantly, Alex shared the peach cobbler with the students.
9. Alex gently lowered a dish of peach cobbler at each place setting.
10. Alex set the dessert bowls of peach cobbler on the table.

YOU ARE WHAT YOU EAT, PAGE 60
Answers will vary. Sample answers:

Allison woke up **and** knew something was wrong. She had always heard the saying, "You are what you eat." **However**, she wasn't prepared for this. **Next,** she whipped back her covers **and** stared down at herself in shock. **Yesterday** she had been a normal girl. **Today** she was a slice of pepperoni pizza.

She couldn't believe her eyes. True, her mother had warned her. She had told her that she should eat healthier food. **However**, she had not paid attention. **But** now that she was an actual slice of pizza, she could see how greasy and fattening she was. **On the other hand**, she really did smell good. "I'm making myself hungry," she thought.

She heard her mom calling her down to breakfast. "Hurry up, **or** you'll be late for school!" **Suddenly**, Allison panicked. What was she supposed to wear to school? **Furthermore**, how was she supposed to fit clothes over pepperoni and cheese?

Meanwhile, Allison's little brother, Leo, was struggling to open his bedroom door. He had been transformed into an ice cream cone, **and** he was melting, fast.

THE FOOD BATTLE, PAGE 61
Answers will vary. Sample answer:

Alexander hated oatmeal. He really, really, really hated oatmeal. **In fact,** he hated it so much he absolutely refused to eat it.

Alexander's mother, **however**, thought oatmeal was very, very, very good for a child, **so** she made it every morning for Alexander. **Therefore**, every morning there was a battle. Alexander whined. He pouted.

He cried. He tried feeding the oatmeal to the cat when his mother wasn't looking. He **also** tried feeding it to his sister, who was only a baby and didn't understand how awful oatmeal tastes.

Once he even slipped some oatmeal into his shoes. He walked with squishy feet to the bathroom and scraped the oatmeal into the toilet. **Then** he flushed it down. He didn't notice that oatmeal had squished out over the top of his shoes and left little drops all the way from the kitchen to the bathroom.

However, his mother was on the lookout for oatmeal tricks. She watched Alexander like a hawk every morning. **Finally,** Alexander gave up. Every morning he sighed, held his nose, and choked it down. He felt full then. He felt sick.

His mother, **though,** felt happy.

ADDING SOME ORDER, PAGE 62

Answers will vary. Sample answer:

Chop a medium onion into very fine pieces. Peel four red potatoes, or just wash them thoroughly if you want to leave the peelings on. Chop the potatoes into one inch cubes. Put the potatoes in a pan and just cover with water. Cook until tender—about 15 minutes. Drain. Meanwhile, cook minced onion in a big pot with some melted butter. Cook until tender and add the drained potatoes. Pour in four to five cups of milk and simmer until it is piping hot. Add salt and pepper at this time. If you prefer thick soup, mix a half cup of cold water and two tablespoons of flour in a cup. Add to the soup. Garnish with a dollop of sour cream and bacon bits, if you wish. Serve.

AUDIENCE, AUDIENCE, AUDIENCE, PAGE 63

Answers will vary. Sample answers:

1. A good friend of yours, in an e-mail:

    Girlfriend! How's it going? Went to that new restaurant, Fire and Ice…so cool! You'll love it. Awesome food. Super cute waiters. OMG, it is the best! But get this. When we were there for Aunt L's birthday, a fire broke out in the kitchen! We had to get out, fast, and the fire department came and everything. Nobody was hurt, but pretty exciting.(The fire fighters were cute, too!)

    Me.

2. The manager of the restaurant, in a letter:

Dear Manager:

The other evening, my family and I dined at your establishment, and we were just starting to eat when suddenly the fire alarm went off. We had to evacuate the restaurant and stand in the cold while the problem was addressed. Although no one was injured and the staff did reheat our dinners, they did not compensate us in any way for the inconvience we experienced. I feel strongly that an adjustment should have been made to our bill, to make up for the disruption to our evening and to my aunt's birthday celebration. I am enclosing a photocopy of our receipt, and I hope you will reimburse us for at least 25% of the cost of the meal.

Sincerely,
Joseph Arlington

4. Your great-grandmother, in a short note on a greeting card:

Dear Granny,

How are you? I hope this card finds you well. I miss you! I wanted to tell you real quick about the excitement we had last night. We all went out to eat last night for Aunt Lydia's birthday. It was a beautiful place with sparkling chandeliers, bright white tablecloths, and fancy silverware. The food was delicious, although not as great as your cooking! Anyway, there was a fire in the kitchen while we were there! Smoke was pouring out, and we all had to evacuate and stand outside in the snow while the fire department put the fire out. Pretty exciting! Don't worry, though. No one was hurt. When you come to visit, we will have to take you there. (And hope there's no fire!)

Love,
Suzanne

ALPHABETICALLY SPEAKING, PAGE 64

Answers will vary. Sample answer:

All of the members of my family—except for me—decided it would be a great idea to go to Ivan's House of Sauerkraut for dinner. **B**ecause the snowstorm I had prayed for didn't happen, there was no other choice but to go.

"**C**ould you have picked a worse place to eat?" I said to my parents.

"**D**on't whine," said Mom.

"**E**very time I give you my opinion, you totally ignore it," I said.

"**F**elicia, that's just not true," said Dad.

Give me a break, I thought. **H**ow was I going to get through the evening at that awful restaurant? **I**t was then that I came up with a plan. **J**amming my coat pockets full of candy bars, I smiled to myself. **K**eeping my coat near me during dinner would be the only hard part.

"**L**et's go!" yelled Dad.

Mom was already waiting in the car.

"**N**ow!" Dad yelled again.

"**O**kay, okay—I'm coming!" I said.

Putting on my candy-laden coat, I rushed down the stairs. **Q**uickly, I ran out of the house, closing the door behind me. **R**ight as I closed it, the bottom of my coat got caught in the door, and all of my candy bars spilled out of my pockets onto the ground.

"**S**omeone is going to spoil their dinner with candy bars!" yelled Dad when he saw me scrambling to pick them up. "**T**oo bad your diabolical plan failed!"

Unable to come up with a lie that would explain the candy bars, I decided to be completely honest. "**V**ariety! **W**hy can't we have some variety! E**x**pect more diabolical plans if you continue making me go to Ivan's House of Sauerkraut! **Y**uck! **Z**ucchini and broccoli milkshakes would be better than that!"

VERBING, PAGE 65

Answers will vary. Sample answers:

1. Fluffikens drank/lapped/guzzled/swallowed/spilled/loved the milk.
2. Ashley drove/wrecked/washed/totaled/parked/cherished the ice cream truck.

3. Elwood invited/despised/adored/annoyed/hugged/called his personal chef.
4. Grandmother cooked/burned/sliced/ate/hid/molded the meat loaf.
5. Someone stole/saved/lost/fed/named/froze the turkey.

RED HERRINGS, PAGE 67

Answers will vary. Sample answers:

1. Red herring: There has just been a warning in the paper about the coffee shop bandit targeting kids.
2. Red herring: The head librarian insists on keeping *Bad Stuff* on the shelves.
3. Red herring: His mother is also in prison for murder and is serving her 25th year of a 55 year sentence.

GOLDILOCKS FOR THE 21ST CENTURY, PAGE 68

Once upon a time, a girl named Goldilocks decided to go for a run on the trail in the forest near the development where she lived. She put on her running shoes and grabbed her mp3 player and was off, listening to her favorite tunes.

After she had been running for about forty-five minutes, she was surprised to see a little cottage nestled in the woods. She didn't know that three bears lived in the cottage—a mama bear, a papa bear, and a baby bear.

Curious, she decided to investigate. She walked up to the cottage and peeked in. No one seemed to be around, but she saw there were three bowls of food sitting on the table. Goldilocks was hungry and decided to climb in the window. Sometimes she didn't make the wisest choices.

She looked at the bowls. "Hmmmm," she said. "It seems to be porridge. I've never tasted porridge before. But I am hungry, so I'll try it." She took a spoonful from the papa bear's bowl. "This is too hot." She took a spoonful from the mama bear's bowl. "This is too cold." She took a spoonful from the baby bear's bowl. "This is just right!" she said. "But it tastes awful!" She swallowed hard and tried not to throw up.

Then she saw three chairs. She was tired from running and decided to rest. She sat in the papa bear's chair. It was too hard. She sat in the mama bear's chair. It was too soft. She sat in the baby bear's chair. It was just right! Unfortunately, Goldilocks was heavier than the baby bear, and the chair broke. "Oops," said Goldilocks. She really was an irresponsible girl sometimes. She shrugged her shoulders and went into the bedroom, where she saw three beds.

She tried the papa bear's bed and the mama bear's bed and found them, just as you might expect, too hard and too soft. "This is quite frustrating," she said. Then she snuggled into the baby bear's bed. "Ahhh.....just right!" she smiled. She tensed up for a moment, worrying that the bed might break. It didn't. She relaxed and fell fast asleep.

In just a little while, the three bears came back from *their* run in the woods.

"I'm tired!" said the baby bear. "I'm starving, too."

"I'm tired of listening to you complain," said Papa Bear. "Sit down and eat your porridge."

"I want Frosted Chocolate Oat Yummies!" said Baby Bear. "Nobody eats porridge anymore!"

"You do," said Mama Bear. "Now hush and take a bite."

Baby Bear looked around for some kind of distraction. He was not going to eat porridge, no matter what. He was thrilled to see that his little chair was broken. He pretended to be upset, but he really wasn't. He thought it was time he got a leather recliner.

"My chair!" cried Baby Bear. "Someone broke it!"

"Is that someone you?" asked Papa Bear suspiciously.

"Would I lie?" Baby Bear put on his most innocent face.

Papa Bear frowned. "I do remember the incident involving the cat and the chocolate pudding...," he started.

"Never mind that, Dad," said Baby Bear. "You look tired. I think it's time we all took a nap."

Papa Bear looked suspicious, but he *was* tired. He agreed, and they all went into the bedroom.

"There's a girl in my bed!" cried Baby Bear.

"What did I tell you about lying?" yelled Papa Bear.

"No, really! Look!"

All three bears crowded around Goldilocks. Just then, she woke up.

"This bad dream seems very real," she murmured, rubbing her eyes.

Papa Bear growled.

"Calm down, dear," said Mama Bear.

Papa Bear growled again.

Goldilocks realized that she was not in a dream. "Ummmmm, I think I'll be going," she said, sitting up.

Papa Bear growled again, very loudly.

Goldilocks was glad she hadn't taken off her running shoes. She leaped out of bed and ran out of that house as fast as she could.

Papa Bear turned to go after her, but Mama Bear grabbed his arm. "Let her go, dear," she said. "You don't need her. We still have all that nice porridge to eat."

APOSTROPHE-ITIS, PAGE 70

1. Special for the day: spinach omelets with cheddar cheese.
2. Satisfaction is guaranteed. We want all customers to leave the Phish Pharm happy.
3. Sign in the kitchen: Each waiter's apron must be clean. Each waiter must wash hands after leaving the rest room. Each waiter's pants must be black. Mrs. Gomez says, "Any waiter whose shirt is not sparkling white and freshly ironed will be sent home to change."
4. The chicken is grilled and served on a bed of romaine lettuce leaves, with our "signature" lemon and artichoke dressing on the side. Waiters sing "That's Amoré" while you eat.
5. We believe that the customer who isn't satisfied is a customer who deserves better. At Penelope's Pie Palace, we do our best to please everyone.
6. Each person's order is treated with the utmost in care. Our chef says, "We want you to come back again and again."
7. Chef Anthony's creations are the talk of the town.
8. We've got pies, cookies, doughnuts, cakes, and other goodies that will make your mouth water.

ANSWER KEY

ANSWER KEY

DAILY BREAD, PAGE 71

Answers will vary. Sample answers:

	B	**R**	**E**	**A**	**D**
Desserts	blueberry pie	rhubarb pie	egg custard	apple pie	date bars
Vegetables	beets	radish	eggplant	asparagus	dill pickle or daikon
Verbs related to cooking or eating	braise	roll	eat	ate	devour
Six-letter food names	bonbon	raisin	eggnog	apples	donuts
Things people normally use in sandwiches	bread	red onion	egg salad	avocado	Dijon mustard
Three-syllable food names	broccoli	raspberry	escargot	apricot	Doritos
Words that might describe a food	baked	ripe	excellent	average	delicious

JELL-O SCULPTURE CONTEST, PAGE 72

1. b
2. a
3. g
4. c
5. d
6. i
7. h
8. f
9. j
10. e

Answers will vary. Sample answers:

1. willy-nilly
2. lollygagging
3. magnanimous
4. flabbergasted
5. flippant
6. mollycoddled
7. flibbertigibbet
8. guffawed

9. bamboozled
10. inconsolable
11. flibbertigibbet

CONFUSING THE CUSTOMERS, PAGE 74

1. d
2. a
3. i
4. f
5. j
6. g
7. h
8. e
9. b
10. c

Answers will vary. Sample answers:

1. flummoxed
2. maligning
3. balderdash
4. prattle
5. squelch
6. candor
7. quibble
8. negligible
9. arduous
10. rapture

SUPPORTING WHAT YOU SAY, PAGE 76

Answers will vary. Sample answers:

1. Subject: Fish make much better pets than cats.
    - Fish don't wander around and aren't easily lost.
    - Fish don't claw your furniture like cats do.
    - Fish don't have litter boxes to clean.

2. Subject: People should be required to go to school until age 30.
    - More people would have jobs because there would be fewer people in the job market.
    - There wouldn't be so much pressure to learn everything by the time a person is 18.
    - If students have children of their own in school, everyone would have the same holidays off.

3. Subject: Children should watch television for at least eight hours a day.

- Children will then appreciate the outdoors much more.
- Children will really appreciate spending time with friends and family after spending so much time with television.
- Children are bound to learn something from the educational programs on television.

4. Subject: Children should not be allowed to watch television at all.
   - Children will use their imaginations more if they aren't allowing television to do all their imagining for them.
   - Children will be able to spend more time building lasting relationships.
   - Children will read more books when they don't have television to fill their time.

REAL NICE, REAL GOOD, PAGE 78

Answers will vary. Sample answers:

Scene #1

It was an exciting game, with the score terrifyingly close until the end of the last quarter. People were on the edge of their seats until the very last minute. We were thrilled that our team won the division championship.

Scene #2

Claire took her little sister to see *Enchanted*. Emma laughed and giggled through the whole show, and Claire loved watching her have such a good time. Afterward, they strolled over to Dairy Delight Ice Cream Palace, where they indulged themselves with decadent hot fudge caramel marshmallow sundaes. They felt so stuffed they were glad to walk the 10 blocks back to the car, just to get some exercise.

Scene #3

Brett visited a well-known, reputable dealership to find a reliable used Honda. He discovered a beauty at an affordable price. Brett's wife loved the hot red paint job, and Brett appreciated the service record and excellent detailing. He made an offer and closed the deal the same day.

Scene #4

Courtney gazed around at the opulent dining room of the 5-star hotel. "This is gorgeous," she thought. "It will have to do," said her sister. Alicia was known for being awfully particular.

"We're going to have the time of our lives here," declared Courtney, imagining herself in her wedding gown next to the gold fountain. "This will be a wedding reception to top them all."

IN OTHER WORDS, PAGE 80

Answers will vary. Sample answer:

Almost everyone has eaten some kind of sausage, but most people probably don't know exactly what is in the sausage and maybe wouldn't want to know. The practice of making sausage started in the days when people were less wasteful. Farmers and butchers tried to find a use for other parts of a pig or other animal besides just the muscle meat. They ground up the organ meat along with meat trimmings and added spices and fillers like fat or even blood. They stuffed the mixture into the intestines of the animal to form sausages.

What the sausage contains depends upon where it is made. In the United States, sausage can't contain more than 50% fat, but in other countries, the fat content can be higher. Also, sausage made in Europe or Asia may contain more starchy fillers than is allowed in the United States. Most sausages today use cellulose or collagen casings, rather than an actual animal intestine. Some even use plastic.

Sausage is common in many countries throughout the world. In Germany, sausage is especially popular with over a thousand varieties. The most common sausages in the U.S. are usually in the form of hot dogs, bratwurst, salami, kielbasa and chorizo.

IN FEWER WORDS, PAGE 81

Answers will vary. Sample answer:

Brutus Fowler won the Cascades County Bake-Off Championship on Saturday with his Dark Chocolate Banana Dreamboat cake. He won $1,000 and 25 pounds of sugar.

Fowler, a tall, muscular man with tattoos of snakes and skulls covering his arms, has been baking cakes since he was 12. That's when he began helping his mother in her bakery. Soon customers were asking for his cakes.

His girlfriend Allison Ginnelli reports that, though Fowler looks like someone you wouldn't want to run into in a dark alley, "He's as gentle as a puppy dog."

PARAPHRASE—AND SUM IT UP, PAGE 82

Answers will vary. Sample answer:

Paraphrased:

When it comes to food, there are a few brave souls who will try anything. Some of them will even try the dangerous, potentially deadly dish fugu, a Japanese dish made from the poisonous pufferfish. It can kill you if it is not cooked properly, causing a slow death by paralysis and suffocation. There is no remedy and most people die in the first 24 hours, though a few people do survive.

In order to know how to cook fugu properly, a chef must have two to three years of training and then pass a rigorous test before being licensed to prepare it. Only about one-third of those who take the test are able to pass it. It is often someone without this special training who tries to cook the fish and then dies from eating it.

There are known cases where poor homeless people found some pufferfish in discarded restaurant food and died from eating it. Now, there are laws that require any leftover parts of the fish to be put into sealed containers and then incinerated. Even the utensils used in the preparation must be kept isolated from other food.

In 1975, a famous actor in Japan ordered four servings of the liver, the most toxic part of the pufferfish. The chef was only trying to accommodate his famous customer, but lost his license after the actor died.

ANSWER KEY

ANSWER KEY

Summarized:

Certain foods can be fatal if prepared incorrectly. One of them is Japanese fugu, which is made from the poisonous pufferfish. It is so dangerous that in Japan it must be prepared by a specially trained, licensed chef. There are even strict laws governing the disposal of leftover parts of the pufferfish. Fugu prepared incorrectly usually results in death by paralysis and suffocation. In one 1975 incident, a chef lost his license after a famous actor ate four servings of pufferfish liver and died.

PERSONIFYING FOOD, PAGE 83

Answers will vary. Sample answers:

1. That bowl of hot chili **kicked** my sinuses into shape.
2. The smell of rotten cheese **knocked** me over.
3. I can hear that tiramisu **whispering** my name
4. Those sizzling hot fajitas are **telling** me to hurry up and eat.
5. The mashed potatoes **hugged** the meat loaf on my crowded plate.

HOW MANY WAYS..., PAGE 84

Answers will vary. Sample answers:

That was a feast for the gods.
My entrée was delectably seasoned and delicious.
The cuisine at Jay's bistro was out of this world.
The food at Farmer's Table rivals my grandmother's cooking.
The gourmet selections were worth their weight in gold.
It's a good thing it was a buffet, because I wanted more of everything.
I couldn't stop eating those tasty appetizers.
Whoever cooked that meal knew that the way to a man's heart is through his stomach.

I found myself taking a nice little nap after about half an hour of that movie.
The plot for that film moved much too slowly to keep my attention
There was not nearly enough action in that flick.
That movie might appeal to a very dull person.
Tonight's feature film sent me off to the land of nod.
That so called "movie" certainly didn't move me.
That film would put a dead person to sleep.

Do they have plastic surgery for dogs?
That mutt would run away from itself if it looked in a mirror.
I've never seen a canine with a more unappealing face.
That dog would never win a beauty contest.

My Heinz 57 mutt certainly isn't a show dog.
That rat terrier looks more like a rat than a dog.
I think that mutt needs a little trip to the beauty parlor.

A SPOT OF PLOT, PAGE 85

Answers will vary. Sample answer:

Zack and Lily loved to cook and loved to search for recipes for something really interesting to **cook**. One night, they decided they wanted a new cookbook, so they went to the bookstore to have a **look**. The bookstore was right next door to an old restaurant that had been closed for a long **time**. The dark, empty building looked kind of creepy and it was hard to imagine that the old restaurant had ever earned a **dime**. Zack and Lily paused in front of the dark and gloomy place and wondered if another restaurant would ever move in **again**. Zack thought that some entrepreneur would eventually think of a new place to open up there, but the question was, "**When**?" While they were standing there, their friend Jason came **along**. As they talked, Jason mentioned that the old restaurant building was for sale and could be bought for not much more than a **song**. He was pushing his dad to buy it and open a cool new hangout for the younger **crowd**. He hoped they could serve burgers, wings and fries and play the music really **loud**. Zack and Lily suggested that Jay and his dad should offer healthier **fare**. Jay thought about that and doubted that the younger crowd would honestly **care**. Zack and Lily offered to devise a menu that would have great **appeal**. Jay promised to talk to his dad and see if they could come up with a **deal**. Since it was getting kind of late, the three shook hands and Zack and Lily went on in to the **bookstore**. They bought five cookbooks and headed home to cook some **more**.

GETTING HYPERBOLIC, PAGE 86

Answers will vary. Sample answers:

If all the cakes in the world were lined up and judged by the greatest food experts in the world, there is no doubt which cake would win. It would be Aunt Eleanor's chocolate decadence cake tower. This cake is not only a delight to look at with its gorgeous, glossy sheen, it is pure heaven to eat. Take one bite, and you are transported into ecstasy.

1. My new kitchen has the shiniest, newest appliances of any kitchen this side of the Mississippi. It's so high tech that Rachel Ray is jealous.
2. My homemade pizza puts any pizza anywhere to shame. Its crust is perfect. The toppings are perfect. The sauce is perfect. The taste is perfect. No one can top this pizza, period.
3. My new job as a celebrity chef is the most wonderful job in the history of the world, and I'm sure every one who cooks must be eyeing me with envy.
4. My baby brother's appetite is so big, he could eat a mountain of peas and then a mountain of cookies for dessert, and he still wouldn't be satisfied.
5. The class I'm taking on gourmet cooking makes me so excited to get up in the morning. I'm filled with happy expectations each morning, and simply in awe of the teacher and all we're learning. No class on any subject has ever been as good as this one.

6. My talent at cooking can't be matched. I'm so good no one gets even close to matching my ability.
7. My friend Alyssa is so efficient at waiting tables, if you blink, you will miss her. She makes all other waitresses look like amateurs.

SYNOPSIS TIME, PAGE 87

Answers will vary. Sample answers:

One evening in a fancy café, one of the customers discovers a body in the men's restroom. The unfortunate victim has been stabbed from behind with a butcher's knife. There is no sign of a struggle and it appears the victim never knew what hit him.

The police, of course, are suspicious of the chef. He had access to knives like the one used in the murder, he had the opportunity since he was at the restaurant all the time and wouldn't arouse suspicion going into the men's restroom, and he has no alibi—he was there at the restaurant all evening. The only thing the police lack is a motive. The chef is a nice guy liked by everyone.

So, who would commit such a terrible crime? One of the customers, an ex-con with a flare for the dramatic, did the dastardly deed and then framed the poor chef. Through many twists and turns, the chief inspector unravels the mystery and brings justice to the murderer, restoring the dignity and reputation of the good chef.

EUPHEMISTICALLY SPEAKING, PAGE 88

1. Grandma, Fufu died.
2. You sure used a lot of big words in your long, boring book without any plot.
3. See next page.

Dear Loving Mother of Seneca,

Seneca is a lively addition to our afternoon story time group. Seneca shares her love of singing with us and her ongoing appreciation of dark chocolate. Her gregarious nature inspires those around her to stand up for one another.

Although Seneca seems to enjoy being in the company of her peers, may I suggest that she will excel in a more energetic setting? The city offers a theatre class that Seneca would be perfect for. I took it upon myself to contact the teacher to tell her all about Seneca's profound ability to touch other people. She was thrilled to hear about such an exuberant young girl who has the natural ability to evoke emotion from those around her. Seneca is signed up for the very next class!

The only hitch is that the theatre class is on the same day and the same time as our story time group. The class is located at 225 North Faraway Lane and the teacher's name is Ms. Openarms. I think you will agree that Seneca will thrive in a more active environment like theatre.

Thank you for your time.

Sincerely,
Ms. Hadenough

ANSWER KEY

PIZZA MONSTER, PAGE 89

Answers will vary. Sample answer:

Plorkapista, the pizza monster, is a hungry dude with an insatiable appetite for pepperoni, sausage and anchovies. He is a hulking figure, around seven feet tall, with huge jowls and a stomach that resembles an enormous wad of pasty-colored dough. We know it's pasty-colored because it sticks out of his red pants—red, the color of tomato sauce. He roams the streets, constantly searching for a pizza opportunity. He steals pizza wherever he can find it: from trashcans, dumpsters, pizza shops, picnic tables and even out of your refrigerator. You can hear him when he approaches because he lumbers along with heavy footsteps. You can smell him even before you hear him because he reeks with the stench of greasy meat and anchovy juice.

However, he's not all bad. He may steal pizza, but he always leaves something behind to replace it. It might be a little bottle of free motel shampoo, a chocolate mint, a can of soda, *something*. Unlike other monsters, Plorkapista has never hurt anyone—he only wants pizza.

FOOD HOUSE, PAGE 90

Answers will vary. Sample answer:

Sienna's apartment door is as heavy as a lasagna and bread dinner. The metal door is a bright red cherry. Her living room feels light yet refreshing like a crisp green salad. The wood floors are graham crackers with soft area rugs like marshmallows. Her painted walls are melted dark chocolate, smooth and comforting. The modern leather furniture is creamy peanut butter spread on green apples. The entire apartment smells sweet, like fresh baked banana bread.

CLICHÉS, PAGE 93

Answers will vary. Sample answer:

"I just made the best cookies I've ever tasted!" said Marcella.

"Well, you're sure **tooting your own horn**," said her sister Carmen. "I'll bet I've made plenty of cookies that are just as good."

"I doubt it. These were special. I threw in **just about everything but the kitchen sink**, so they **cost an arm and a leg**. They may be expensive, but they are definitely worth it."

"Let's have a contest. Let's both bake another batch, and if my cookies aren't as good as yours, I'll **eat my hat**." Carmen was **madder than a wet hen**. She hated how her sister was always bragging. "I could beat her **with one hand tied behind my back**," she thought to herself.

"Could I get **a word in edgewise**?" interrupted their mother. "I hate to **rain on your parade**, but we are not having a cookie cooking contest in this kitchen. If you two **have time on your hands**, I've got three closets that need to be cleaned, and **many hands make light work**, you know."

The girls looked at each other. "**Hold your horses**, Mom," said Carmen. "We were just kidding around. Let's not **make a mountain out of a molehill**."

"Let's put that contest **on the back burner** for now," said Marcella.

"Well, no one can ever say you two **work your fingers to the bone**," said Mom.

Without clichés:

"I just made the best cookies I've ever tasted!" said Marcella.

"Well, you're sure not shy about giving yourself credit," said her sister Carmen. "I'll bet I've made plenty of cookies that are just as good."

"I doubt it. These were special. I threw in a whole cupboard full of ingredients, so they are probably the priciest cookies you'll ever see. They may be expensive, but they are definitely worth it."

"Let's have a contest. Let's both bake another batch, and if my cookies aren't as good as yours, I'll do a big favor for you—whatever you like." Carmen was so angry her hands were shaking and she felt sure that Marcella could see smoke coming out of her brain. She hated how her sister was always bragging. "I could beat her if I made my cookies while blindfolded," she thought to herself.

"Could I have my say?" interrupted their mother. "I hate to destroy the fun you are obviously having by trying to out-cook one another, but we are not having a cookie cooking contest in this kitchen. If you two have nothing better to do, I've got three closets that need to be cleaned. If we all get started on them together, they'll be finished in no time."

The girls looked at each other. "Let's not rush things, Mom," said Carmen. "We were just kidding around. We were just exaggerating and didn't mean a thing by our joshing around."

"Let's forget about that contest for now," said Marcella.

"Well, no one can ever say you two are hard workers," said Mom, "although you may be fast thinkers."

WATCHING A CHARACTER, PAGE 94

Answers will vary. Sample answer:

Lula jammed her fork into the lasagna and scooped up a dripping chunk of pasta. Shoving it into her mouth, she began to chew noisily.

"This stuff is nothing but grease," she complained, and reached for another bite. "You really ought to learn how to cook."

Wiping her mouth on her shirt, she stood up, reached over, and cut off another chunk. She plopped the new chunk on her plate, sat down, and stabbed again. "Way, way too greasy," she said. "I'd never serve a lasagna like this to my guests."

STRAIN YOUR BRAIN #1, PAGE 95

Answers will vary. Sample answer:

1. An aardvark, anteater and monkey ate many apples, mangoes and artichokes at Mickey's Mansion.
2. There are several different kinds of pasta: spaghetti, ravioli, linguini and fettuccini to name a few. Somehow I always thought pasta meant only spaghetti. Then my friend Linny told me about linguini, while Ralph introduced me to ravioli. So the next time my friends came over for dinner, my mom prepared spaghetti, but used the wrong noodles! Susan told her that spaghetti was a round noodle and what she used was fettuccini. All my friends were staring at their plates, but Finnegan felt foolish looking at the fettuccini. So he said, "Does it really matter? It still tastes yummy!"
3. My least favorite job is mowing the lawn. We have such a stupid **lawn mower**! There's no motor on it, so you just have to push and push and push. It takes forever to finish the lawn. Usually, when it is my turn

to mow, I stock up on food to have when I need a break. So, yesterday, I loaded up the patio table with a **banana**, a plate of cold **spaghetti,** and iced tea with a slice of **lemon**. Before I started to mow, I also got out the **blender** and made a strawberry smoothie to carry around with me. It was terrific. As I walked back outside, I saw my Dad standing in front of the mower. Was I surprised when he stepped aside and displayed a new motorized **lawn mower**! He yanked the rope and the engine sputtered then **purred** as it kicked into gear. I was ecstatic. I mowed the lawn in record time and watched my dad eat my lunch treat on the patio as I mowed!

4. As he sipped chai tea, Marvin waited for his cell phone to ring.
   Sally made obnoxious slurping sounds as she sipped the last of her peppermint milkshake.
   Mack sipped his soda from a 96-ounce cup from the convenience store as he barreled down the highway.

5. Have you tried Plinkmottle? If not, it's time you did. Grab your straw. Grab your sweet tooth. Grab a glass. Then pour. The iridescent green color will tantalize your tastebuds, and you will start sipping. And sipping. And sipping. Then you'll say what everyone says: More Plinkmottle, please!

STRAIN YOUR BRAIN #2, PAGE 96

Answers will vary. Sample answer:

1. I love chocolate. Dark chocolate is best. It satisfies my sweet tooth. I especially like gooey chocolate brownies. There is a health benefit called antioxidants. Antioxidants inhibit reactions of cancer causing free radicals.
2. There were smelly feet by her bed.
3. Milk is a food. You can drink it plain or add stuff to it. It tastes best if it's cold. My day is off to a good start if I have a long drink of milk. Want some?
4. Butter. Left-over spaghetti. Orange juice. Eggs. Lettuce. Cream cheese. Ketchup. Milk.
5. Butter melted all over the place when the refrigerator lost power.
   Left-over spaghetti rotted at the very back of the refrigerator.
   Orange juice, combined with some strawberries and some yogurt, makes a great smoothie.
   Eggs and broccoli taste great in broccoli quiche.
   Lettuce earns "boos" when it is on the menu at our house.
   Cream cheese enhances the flavor of a bagel.
   Ketchup complements a hamburger nicely.
   Milk and cookies make a wonderful snack.

BARE BONES, PAGE 97

Answers will vary. Sample answers:

1. The crowd in the hockey arena stared in disbelief as the angry fan tossed his hamburger, his super-sized root beer, and an open bag of M&M's onto the ice, causing a massive pile-up of players, hockey sticks, and referees.
2. Hancock proudly cooked his own dinner for the first time, opening a Big Guy frozen pizza and slipping it, plastic covering and all, into the oven.

3. Grandmother carefully placed a spoonful of mashed potatoes on each plate, followed by a teaspoonful of gravy, three carrots, and the thinnest slice of meat loaf anyone had ever seen.
4. Jake looked back and forth between the asparagus on his plate and his mother's warning eyes and finally decided that choking down one bite was smarter than spitting it out onto their neighbor's white lace tablecloth.
5. The Hartwick's babied their little tomato plants, washing their leaves, spraying them for bugs, and talking to them every evening before they went to bed.

COMPOUNDS, PAGE 98

Answers will vary. Sample answers:

1. Henry and Billy ate the chocolate covered grasshoppers.
2. Henry ate the chocolate covered grasshoppers and then threw up.
3. Henry ate the chocolate covered grasshoppers, but his sister knew better.

1. compound sentence
2. compound sentence
3. compound subject
4. compound sentence
5. no compounds
6. compound sentence with compound subjects and compound predicates
7. no compounds
8. compound sentence
9. compound sentence
10. compound subject
11. compound predicate
12. compound sentence with compound predicates
13. no compounds
14. compound sentence with a compound predicate
15. no compounds

IN THE NEWS, PAGE 100

Answers will vary. Sample answer:

A boa constrictor got loose in the lunch room at Sternbladt Junior High on Friday morning. The snake escaped because someone left its cage door open. Students panicked when they spotted the snake in the cafeteria. The snake made its way into the kitchen, where it was cornered and caught by the science teacher and the gym teacher. No one was injured in the incident.

MS. PERSNICKETY NEEDS HELP, PAGE 103

Answers will vary. Sample answer:

Last week in the school cafeteria, we had **quiet alot** of excitement. The members of the school board came to visit on the day the new menu was introduced. **Me and my friends** were **their** when the board members arrived and they looked **kinda** hungry. **So** the principal came in to show them the new menu. **Well,** it has all kinds of healthy choices on **it, as** soon as **I seen** it I knew I wouldn't like it.

So the principal goes, "**Your gonna** be so pleased with our new, healthy food items. We have all sorts of fruits and fresh vegetables **and stuff**." We **use to** have more fast food, chips, cookies, **ect**. on the menu which **supposebly** isn't very good for us.

Well, of course the school board members liked it. They were **especially** pleased with the salad bar because I think they want to **loose** some weight. That doesn't mean we want to **loose** some weight, though. **Its alright** with me if they want to go on a diet, but **its** sure not something I want **too** do.

So the school board members each gave a speech **'cuz** they were so happy with the new menu. It was so boring I just wanted to **excape &** all I could think of was that I **shoulda** gone out for lunch. "**Who's** idea was this?" I asked my friend.

"Not mine," he **goes, then** he **lead** me right out of there.

I lied about **they're** being **alot** of excitement. There really wasn't any excitement at all.

MS. PERSNICKETY GETS TESTY, PAGE 104

Answers will vary. Sample answer:

"There's a dead mouse in my soup!" cried Mr. Evanovitch. He thought he was going to throw up. "In fact, there are two dead mice in my soup," he added. " They're both kind of gray and sort of shriveled up."

"I don't think it's especially disgusting," said the waiter, whose name was Charles, as he peered into the soup. He said, "It's certainly nothing to lose your lunch over. We get a lot of mice in the soup here."

Mr. Evanovitch certainly wasn't too happy to hear that. In fact, he was so shocked he just couldn't believe it and didn't know what to say for a moment. "My friends and I have wanted to come here for a long time. Supposedly this is one of the best restaurants in town. I've always heard it was quite nice, but it's certainly not."

"The soup may not be so good, but we've got the best desserts in town," said Charles. "No mice in the desserts at all. If you'd like for me to get you one, I'll be happy to."

Mr. Evanovitch was horrified. "I can't believe I saw mice in my soup, and you aren't even upset. I want to see the manager!"

"All right," said Charles. "I don't think she'll be too happy, though. She's got a lot of work to do." So he went off to find Mrs. Hampshire, who was in her office in the back. He told her what happened and how he felt about it.

"I know I'm supposed to run right out there," sighed Mrs. Hampshire, "but what I'd really like to do is escape. I could really use a hot bath, a massage, a warm cup of cocoa, etc. It's no fun being the manager sometimes. I should have been a nurse. I used to like science and math in school. I would have been happier, I think, as a nurse." She looked at Charles and sighed again. "I know I have to go out there." She got up, and Charles led her out front to Mr. Evanovitch.

Mr. Evanovitch was so upset he couldn't even speak. He just made funny noises in his throat.

"How about a nice piece of pie?" said Mrs. Hampshire. She gave him her most winning smile.

ANSWER KEY

ANSWER KEY

DDN SHOW, PAGE 105

Answers will vary. Sample answers:

1. Midnight Cake—A dark chocolate cake has black licorice whips interlaced across the top to create a lattice look. The cake is served on a chocolate brown plate placed on a black tablecloth. Around the edge of the cake are dozens of tiny black licorice jelly beans. The whole effect is very, very dark and grim.

2. Slime Soup—Spinach cooked until it is very soft is pureed with yellow peppers to create a thick, yellow-green soup. The soup is served in a unique nose-shaped bowl created just for the pleasure of the viewing audience.

3. Prairie Dog Delight—Tomato juice, broccoli, milk, and chicken stock are whirled in a blender to create a healthy brown drink that exactly resembles the brown of a prairie dog's fur. It is served in squat, clear glass tumblers set into a small sandbox.

4. Gravy Soup—Creamy chicken gravy is studded with bits of artichoke heart and mushrooms, creating a thick, lumpy soup. It is to be served in beige bowls with only a big spoon at the side—no placemats, tablecloths, or colorful dishes. A celery stick will be placed in the center of each bowl to stick straight up, showing the thick, richness of the gravy.

5. Chunky Dairy Shake. Milk is whirled in a blender with marshmallows to create a thin milkshake with little lumps in it. The shake has spoonfuls of cottage chesse plopped on top as a garnish. Each milkshake is served in a glass tumbler that will highlight the lumps. Ideally, it should be served alongside the Gravy Soup.

TOPIC AND SUBTOPIC INDEX

Topics and subtopics covered in *Language Is Served* activities are listed below, along with the titles and page numbers of the associated activities.

(continued)

TOPIC INDEX, CONTINUED

ABOUT THE AUTHOR

Cheryl Miller Thurston taught English and writing classes for more than 13 years, grades seven through university. She is the author of many plays, musicals, and books for teachers. She lives with her husband and pampered cats in Colorado.

MORE GREAT BOOKS FROM COTTONWOOD PRESS

A TO Z—Novel Ideas for Reading Teachers. Written by two reading teachers with years of experience in the classroom, the activities in *A to Z* can be used with any novel or short story.

IF THEY'RE LAUGHING THEY JUST MIGHT BE LISTENING—Ideas for Using Humor in the Classroom—Even If You're NOT Funny Yourself." Discover ways to lighten up, encourage humor from others, and have fun with your students.

A SENTENCE A DAY—Short, Playful Proofreading Exercises to Help Students Avoid Tripping Up When They Write. This book focuses on short, playful, interesting sentences with a sense of humor.

PHUNNY STUPH—Proofreading Exercises with a Sense of Humor. The activities contain just about every error you can imagine, from spelling and punctuation mistakes to sentence fragments and run-ons.

DOWNWRITE FUNNY—Using Students' Love of the Ridiculous to Teach Serious Writing Skills. The entertaining activities and illustrations in this book help teach all kinds of useful writing skills.

RELUCTANT DISCIPLINARIAN—Advice on Classroom Management from a Softy Who Became (Eventually) a Successful Teacher. Author Gary Rubinstein offers clear and specific advice for classroom management.

HOT FUDGE MONDAY—Tasty Ways to Teach Parts of Speech to Students Who Have a Hard Time Swallowing Anything To Do With Grammar. This new edition includes quirky quizzes, extended writing activities, and Internet enrichment activities that reinforce new skills.

THINKING IN THREES—The Power of Three in Writing. Faced with a writing task of any kind? Think of three things to say about the topic. Writing an essay? Remember that the body should have at least three paragraphs. Need help getting started? Learn three ways to begin an essay.

HOW TO HANDLE DIFFICULT PARENTS—A Teacher's Survival Guide. Suzanne Capek Tingley identifies characteristics of some parent "types." She then goes on to give practical, easy-to-implement methods of working with them more effectively.

TWISTING ARMS—Teaching Students How to Write to Persuade. This book is full of easy-to-use activities that will really sharpen students' writing and organizational skills.

COTTONWOOD PRESS INC.

www.cottonwoodpress.com